# Simply Success

# Simply Success

## How to Start, Build, and Grow a Multimillion-Dollar Business—the Old-Fashioned Way

*Jack Miller*

**WILEY**

John Wiley & Sons, Inc.

Published by John Wiley & Sons, Inc., Hoboken, New Jersey.
Published simultaneously in Canada.

*Library of Congress Cataloging-in-Publication Data:*

Miller, Jack, 1929–
   Simply success: how to start, build, and grow a multimillion dollar business the old-fashioned way/ Jack Miller.
      p.   cm.
   ISBN 978-0-470-22452-6   (cloth)

1. New business enterprises.   2. Success in business.   3. Small business.
I. Title.

HD62.5.M54   2008
658.1′1—dc22                                                                 2007033367

Printed in the United States of America.

10  9  8  7  6  5  4  3  2  1

*I dedicate this book to my brother Harvey and my late brother Arnold without whose abilities, encouragement, and constant support Quill could not have become as successful as it did. I also thank them for their friendship and camaraderie, which made the journey so enjoyable.*

*Also, I would like to dedicate it to my late wife Audrey, whose constant support and understanding made it possible for me to spend so much time building Quill. In the last month of her life, I said, "Honey, I wish I could have given you more." Her reply was, "Jack, you gave me what I wanted most, security."*

*And so, building a great business has many different benefits.*

*Also, I dedicate this book to my wife, Goldie, who supported me so much throughout the long task of writing it.*

*And, finally, to my daughters, Judith and Sheri, who have grown up to be fine women in spite of my not being there for their every school event and who have listened to my endless talk about business.*

# Acknowledgments

A heartfelt thank-you to:

My father, for taking all those phone calls in the beginning and for his constant support. (Although years later we heard a story from one of his wholesale customers who said that one day as I was just starting, when my father called on him, the customer said, "Ben, you seem to be downcast." My father replied, "Yes, my son, who has a college degree, wants to sell pencils." I think he pictured me as standing on a street corner with a cup full of pencils. But he never said that to me and never, ever did anything but support us.)

And then I would like to thank my father in law, Jerry Weil, who lent me the $2,000 to get started and then wouldn't take interest on the money when I paid it back six years later. I also appreciate his constant efforts to get us business as he called upon his accounts in the wholesale meat business.

And, Jerry's brother, "Uncle" Herb, who let us use his basement for our first office and who also promoted us to his customers.

Thanks go to my lifelong friend (since fifth grade) and my partner in an acrobatic act in college, Howard I. Bernstein, who was our accountant from day one and who represented us in the sale of the business 43 years later (he had since become a partner in an investment banking firm). He gave us great advice when he was our accountant and he did a masterful job representing us in the sale to Staples. Also, he gave us our first order (for about $6.93). He is a great friend and a terrific business advisor.

I would also like to thank all of the Quill people whose hard work and dedication to our business principles did so much through the years to make Quill the great company it became. From the janitor on through to the top people, every one of them made a contribution to Quill's success. It couldn't have happened without them.

And, finally, I would like to thank all of our loyal Quill customers. Even today, when people ask me what I did for a living and I tell them that my brothers and I owned Quill Corporation, I often get a reply something like; "Quill, oh, I used to (or do) buy from them. I was buying from them when they were back on Belmont Avenue. What a great company. What fantastic service. I got my order almost before I hung up the phone," etc. What a sense of pride that gives me.

So, yes, we did it. But not without a great deal of help and support.

# Contents

Introduction    1

Chapter 1.    A Bit of History    5

Chapter 2.    What It Takes to Be an Entrepreneur    27

Chapter 3.    Getting Started    33

Chapter 4.    Financing    39

Chapter 5.    The Miracle of Hard Work    47

Chapter 6.    The Magic of a Vision    53

Chapter 7.    Focus: Putting on the Blinders    61

Chapter 8.    Concentrate on Your Customer    71

Chapter 9.    There is a Better Way    79

Chapter 10.    Plotting Your Course with Strategic Planning    85

Chapter 11.    Implementation: Making It Happen    91

Chapter 12.    Forecasting and Budgeting    99

Chapter 13.    Using Your Financial Statements to Get Where You Want to Go    105

Chapter 14.    You Can, Too, Argue with Success!    111

Chapter 15.    Building a Great Corporate Culture    117

Chapter 16.    Shaping a Winning Organization    133

Chapter 17.    Who Controls Your Life?    147

Chapter 18.    Easing the Burden    153

Chapter 19.    Doing More by Doing Less    159

Chapter 20.    Your Growth as a Leader    165

Chapter 21.    Someone Changed the Rules. Why Wasn't It Me?    173

Chapter 22.  About the Lifelong Learning Process   179

Chapter 23.  The Art of Survival   185

Chapter 24.  How to Do Almost Everything Wrong   191

Chapter 25.  About Advisors and Boards   203

Chapter 26.  A Family Business Can Be Great—or . . .   209

Chapter 27.  The Glory of the Free Enterprise System   215

Index   219

# Introduction

Being a successful entrepreneur is not all that complex—which is not to say that it is easy. There is a distinct difference between something being simple and something being easy. When I say that being a successful entrepreneur is not complex, I mean that there are some very basic guidelines that are relatively easy to understand and that, when followed, can lead to pretty good success in business. But, that is not to say that these guidelines are easy to implement. It takes a lot of hard work, and, for most of us, a lot of time.

What I attempt to do in writing this book is to introduce and discuss the principles and guidelines we learned over 43 years that helped us grow from a one-man operation, starting with no customers and no sales, into an over-1,200-person operation with close to 800,000 customers and over $630,000,000 in sales . . . all starting with $2,000 borrowed from my father-in-law and with a phone in Dad's live poultry store.

My hope is that some of what I learned will help other entrepreneurs become (more) successful in their own businesses. And perhaps one or more of those entrepreneurs might be my own grandchildren. Nothing could make me prouder than being able to say, "my grandson (or granddaughter), the entrepreneur." For me it has been such a wonderful experience, such a great journey, that I could only wish such a thing for my own grandchildren.

This book is not intended to be a well-researched academic journal. It is simply meant to illustrate the lessons I have learned over 43 years as an entrepreneur, which, by itself, is pretty extensive research. And although I read a great deal about business and attended many seminars over the years, most of these lessons were learned and really driven home by trial-and-error experience. The reading and the seminars helped to sensitize us to many of the issues, but it was only the actual experience that really drove the lessons home. (Or, as my father used to say to my brothers and me, "If you could only learn from my experiences, your life would be easier.")

Believe me, learning from the experience of others is an easier route to take. So, I highly recommend doing as much reading as possible relating to business in general and to your own field in particular. And I truly believe in attending good seminars and talking to other business people. But even after doing all of that and after reading this book, you are going to have to go through the experiences yourself. Hopefully, as you do, a light will go on in your brain and you will say to yourself, "Oh, so that is what he was talking about." Hopefully, the ideas put forth in this book will make your "on the job" learning experience faster . . . and easier. I'm not sure I could hope for much more.

The ideas I will be discussing are, I believe, basic to all businesses, large and small. However, I also believe that they are often ignored, in whole or in part, by a great many businesspeople, from those heading one- or two-man companies on through those heading multibillion-dollar companies. And that amazes me.

Something as simple, and as much talked about, as good customer service, is one of the most ignored. For example, try calling some of your biggest companies, particularly those in the communications area, and try talking to a human being without going through four, five, or six cycles of, "If you want this, press 1, if you want that, press 2," and so on. By the time you get to talk to someone, if you ever do, you are frustrated and annoyed. Service is needlessly, but too often, sacrificed first in a drive for efficiency.

Incidentally, this is why I believe it is probably easier to start and build a company today than when I started. I have never experienced so much plain bad customer service as I do now when dealing with some of these big companies. Top management of these companies talk about good customer service, but I sometimes think that they and those under them, who are implementing the policies, don't even know how to spell the words. You should never be concerned about having to compete with one of the giants, if you focus on providing great customer service.

So, "fanatical" customer service, as a competitor of mine tagged it (why didn't I think of that?), will be one of the topics discussed. And perhaps the word "fanatical" would be a good word to attach to almost all the ideas I will present. "Fanatical" focus, "Fanatical" commitment, "Fanatical" employee support, and so on.

Customer service, focus, commitment, employee support . . . none of these concepts, and others I will talk about, are new or unknown. But, they are often (many usually) ignored. And the concept of being "fanatical" about them is probably what separates the big successes from the also-rans. None of these ideas are new or revolutionary.

I think we are past the craziness of the late 1990s when some of us who had been around for awhile were repeatedly told that this was a "new economy" and the old rules didn't apply any longer. Well, suddenly in 2000, 2001, 2002, and so on we learned that the old rules *did* apply. The crash of the high techs that followed the new rules and ridiculed the old ones just verified the truth of the old saying that, "The old truths, just because they are old and well-known, are none the less true."

In this book I will be presenting some of these "old truths" that we followed faithfully and that helped us build Quill. And, frankly, I believe it is as easy or perhaps even easier (because of better distribution systems and because of new advances such as a small laptop computer that gives you all the computing power you need to compete with the biggest guys) to be successful today as compared with when I started. In fact, because so many businesses don't observe some of the simple rules, it is, possibly, even easier. And don't let the size of competitors scare you, particularly if they are public companies. Their very size (and their being public, if they are) makes them easier targets. You may not want to meet them head on, but you sure can take pretty good chunks of business from them (which they may not even notice) by specializing in some particular niche (another chapter in the book).

In any event, it is going to be all up to you. And with that thought, let me end this introduction by quoting a poem that I like a lot.

> Isn't it strange that princes and kings,
> And clowns that caper in sawdust rings,
> And common folk like you and me.
> Are builders for eternity.
>
> To each is given a set of rules,
> A shapeless mass and a bag of tools.
> And each must make, ere life has flown,
> A stumbling block or a stepping stone.

Hopefully this book, and other reading and listening you do, will give you some of the rules. Your own ability and drive are your set of tools. My wish for you is that, "ere life has flown," and it does fly by quickly, that you have made a wonderful "stepping stone" for yourself, your family, and the world about you.

Good luck.

Jack Miller

# Chapter 1

# A Bit of History

When I first started Quill in 1956, it was with a phone in Dad's chicken store so that he or my uncle Abe could answer it while I was out on the street selling. Many a customer was surprised to hear chickens squawking in the background when they called to place an order.

When a customer called to order office products, in the background they heard any number of odd sounds, at least odd for an office supply company—clucking and squawking, the whomp of the cleaver falling.

In 1998, when we sold Quill to Staples—a terrific, publicly traded company, by the way—our revenues were over $630 million. We had a complete state-of-the-art distribution center of 350,000 square feet on a wooded 35-acre campus plus nine other distribution centers around the country and more than 1,200 employees.

This book is not about Quill but, more importantly, about the lessons we learned along the way in how to build and run a successful company. It's the story of what hard work, reinvesting every penny possible back into the business, and having a passion for what you are doing can lead to.

It has been a great trip, a fabulous trip, and along the way I've learned a lot about business, most of which you don't learn in an Ivy League MBA program. In fact, to tell the truth, I'm not all that impressed with all those Ivy League MBAs, at least not when it comes to building a business. If your goal is to make lots of money in the various financial dealings or to "flip" companies—simply making money without ever creating anything substantial—then this book isn't for you. Get yourself to a bookstore—there are lots of books about making money while building nothing substantial. And perhaps an Ivy League MBA is for you. But if your goal, your dream, is to build a business, to make a good living, maybe one day a great living, without having to work for anyone else, then this book can help. This book is for those entrepreneurs and would-be entrepreneurs who may start out with the modest desire of making a living for themselves and their families and, with the right approach, may surprise themselves (as I did) by ending up with a huge company worth a lot of money, while earning a very good living along the way.

There are millions of entrepreneurs in this country, men and women starting and running the businesses that keep our economy churning—landscaping companies, restaurants, construction firms, caterers, consultants of all sorts, manufacturers, distributors, and on and on. (In fact, of the 25,000,000 or so businesses in the United States, only 20 percent have employees, and of these, 89.3 percent have fewer than 20 employees.) All of these men and women have one thing in common: they are willing to take a risk because they want to work for themselves, believe in making it on their own, and have the self-confidence to do so.

They have something else in common: they are the spirit and the future of America. I know that sounds a bit cliché, but it's true. There are few men and women today who can legitimately claim to wear the mantle of our founders and of the American revolutionaries, as readily as U.S. entrepreneurs. We create jobs. We keep the economy humming. We pay taxes, lots of taxes, and we do it all (except the taxes) on our terms.

Also, like the relatively few giant oaks that grow from some of the millions of tiny acorns, our future huge corporations will spring from some of the millions of small entrepreneurs of this country. (As a side note, yes, I am a cheerleader for U.S. small businessmen and women. That's because I love this country and the opportunity it has given me to achieve to my greatest potential. I want to preserve that opportunity for my children and grandchildren.) One of the things I am doing in my retirement is working to get the teaching of America's founding principles and history into our educational system, particularly on college campuses, where it is much neglected. These are the principles that, among other things, allow and encourage entrepreneurship. When you start a business, three things can eventually happen: the business provides a good living for you and your family; the business grows into a substantial company that you eventually sell or leave in the hands of a successor; or the business fails. The lessons I have learned over more than 43 years may be able to help you increase the odds of the first two outcomes.

I didn't start with a business plan. I started with a need and desire to make a living. It was June 1,1956. I had no job. I had a new wife and a $15,000 mortgage (remember this was 50 years ago, so that was a lot of money).

I had been working at one job or another since I was thirteen. I had been a soda jerk in a drugstore, like in the old movies where you could sit at the counter and order a milkshake. I was a delivery boy for a dry cleaner, an usher at a movie theater, a pin setter at a bowling alley. At fifteen, I drove a small truck for a food distributor.

When I entered college, I was able to pass proficiency tests for two courses (college algebra and Rhetoric 101) thus entering the University of Illinois with six credit hours. I then rushed through college by taking 21 hours a semester instead of the normal 15. I paid my way through school by modeling for art classes, washing dishes, and in the summers digging ditches and loading freight cars. My best friend, who later became my accountant and trusted advisor, and I also had a hand balancing act and we performed in clubs, theaters, and county fairs.

When I graduated three and a half years after I entered, I had no idea what I wanted to do. I thought I might want to be a lumberjack, so I drove a car from Chicago to Portland, Oregon, for a car dealer. By the time I got there, I decided I didn't want to be a lumberjack and I took a train back home. But it was a great trip, still one of my fondest memories.

Still not knowing what I wanted to do, I worked in Dad's live poultry store, slaughtering chickens and cleaning their droppings off the pans below their cages. Since then, I've always felt that was a good way to bring a college graduate back to reality. After a few months, I took a job with a suburban newspaper, selling advertising. But after I found out that the owner was lying about his circulation figures, I quit and with nothing else in mind, I went to work for my brother Arnold (who many years later joined us at Quill) in his "cut up" chicken store. One day, an uncle of ours stopped in at the store while I was mopping the floor. "What kind of job is that for a college graduate?" he asked. Then he offered me a job selling for his company, where they manufactured soup concentrates and gelatin desserts for restaurants, hotels, hospitals, and other institutions.

For the next five years, I traveled the country, often being on the road for five or six weeks, then back for a few days and out on the road again. I worked with our representatives in the field who called on distributors and often worked directly with the distributors calling on the restaurants and institutions. What great training this turned out to be. And what a tremendous bird's-eye view I received on how distribution worked in our country. On top of that, my uncle, who was small compared to his main competitor, focused on extreme customer service, something we later emphasized very strongly at Quill.

But after four years, I got married and after another year on the road, home only for a few days every other week or so, I decided that this was no way to have a married life. So I left my uncle and joined a small firm making custom sample cases for salesmen and distributing briefcases made by others. When I joined the company, we set up the distribution portion of the company as a separate division with me as president, with a 25 percent ownership payable from future profits.

The distribution division was basically a mail order operation plus some direct selling (done by me) in the Chicago area. I began to learn something about mail order and began to build some contacts with businesses in the Chicago area. But a year after I started there, the owner decided to sell the company, including my division. I didn't want to stay with the new owners, whom I didn't trust, so once again I was looking for a career path—not realizing that all the experience I had gotten in the past six years had already put me on that path.

I started applying for various jobs but didn't much care for what I saw. At one firm I evidently failed a psychological test and also asked for too much money. I suspect the test showed that I wouldn't be someone who would follow orders too readily.

In any event, I decided to go into business for myself. But what business? After some thought, I decided that since I had been personally selling briefcases to businesses in the Chicago area, I could still do that. But I knew that was not enough to build a business on. So what else did businesses buy that I could sell? Office supplies seemed an obvious answer.

I thought about buying a small dealer, but I didn't have any money to do it, and besides, I didn't want to have a retail store, which is what most of the small dealers had. I checked around and found a company that had just started a wholesale division selling to dealers. They had a rule that they would sell only to stocking dealers, but with some persuasion, they waived that rule for me. If I would put up a $300 deposit, they would sell to me and even give me some catalogs to distribute to customers.

I borrowed $2,000 from my father-in-law, put a phone in my dad's live poultry store, had some business cards printed, and was off and running. I was in business! I had no business plan. I had no sense of how big the office products industry was or how big the potential market was. I didn't have a line on my competition. I just had a commitment to build a business.

From that to a nationwide over $630 million business with over 1,200 employees in nine distribution centers around the country when we sold the business 43 years later, is the story of Quill and of a great life and a wonderful partnership with my brothers Harvey, who joined me a year and a half after I started and Arnold, who joined us 20 years later.

We built a great company based on unwavering integrity, hard work, and, to borrow a phrase from one of my competitors, a passion for "fanatical customer service." It's a company that went on to even greater success after we sold under the leadership of the team we had built, which Staples was smart enough to leave in charge (keeping the young Harvard MBAs they liked to hire out). Now, nine years later, they are doing more than a billion dollars in volume and are a major contributor to Staples' profits.

Every new business venture is a risk. You can't become an entrepreneur if you are really allergic to risk. In my experience, there are two types of entrepreneurs: those who notice the risk but don't let it bother them too much and those who don't even notice the risk. I was one of the ones who didn't notice the risk. Thinking back, I realized I should have, with a mortgage to pay and a still-new bride. But I guess, from soda jerk to pin setter to standing on my hands at county fairs to traveling the country selling soup concentrates and gelatin desserts, I had come to realize I could always make a living. Now I wanted to make it on my terms.

And maybe part of not worrying about the risk was being young—I was twenty-seven—and having no children. But I've known lots of men and women who have started businesses in their thirties, forties, even fifties. Risk is just a natural part of starting, building, and running a business.

However, and here is the first lesson, once Quill was up and running, we never "bet the entire ranch" on anything we did. We never overextended ourselves. If we couldn't afford to pay for something and move on if it failed, we didn't do it. We always were willing to risk some or all of the profits, but never the company itself.

Let me add a quick word about failure. Some businesses fail. That's as natural as the fact that some seed never sprout or that trees in the forest never grow beyond saplings and even some big ones die. It's just the way life is. There's some possibility your business might fail—though I believe if you read the rest of this book and pick up some of the lessons I'm trying to share, it will be a lot less likely.

But if you want to be an entrepreneur, you can't allow the fear of failure to stop you from trying. No man or woman who honestly started and ran a business has ever really been a failure. Their businesses may have failed, but that's different. Relatively speaking, very few men and women out there have what it takes to try to make it on their own, have the guts and the confidence to say, "I'm going to start my own business. I'm done counting on somebody else for my paycheck!" Somebody like that, while maybe their business might fail, they as a person are not a failure. Anybody who has ever started a business and has done so honestly and with integrity, no matter how it ends up, can look in the mirror knowing that he or she did something few other Americans are able and willing to do.

If you never try, you will never know if you can succeed. But if you do try—and succeed—it is one of the greatest things you can do, in my opinion, even better than winning a gold medal at the Olympics.

So now, on to the history of Quill. First, the name. Why did I choose the name Quill Office Products? Remember what I said about American revolutionaries and independence and doing things on my own terms? When I decided to start my own business, my wife and I went to my best friend's home for dinner. We agreed we would not leave until we had come up with a good name. After hours of discussion, we decided on Quill because the Declaration of Independence was signed with a quill pen and I would be selling pens—along with thousands of other items. Years later, I learned that a name is really what you make it through the company you run and how you run it. Many other names could have worked as well, but I still like our choice.

On June 1, 1956, Quill Office Products was officially open. The very first thing I did that day was to go to the bank. Not to get a loan—I'm not very high on borrowing money, doing so only two times over the life of our business and then for only a few months each time. But my old partner in the briefcase business had advised me that I needed a good relationship with the bank as time went on. So I brought my opening financial statement showing no sales and a balance sheet that showed one used Ford and $2,000 in cash and showed it to a nice older gentleman who was assigned to be in charge of my account. And every month for the next 43 years we always gave the bank a copy of our financials. This is one piece of advice I would like to pass on. Get the bank involved with your business—the good and the ugly. They become your ally.

Then, with the wholesaler's catalog under my arm, I started knocking on doors. I started out with what I thought was a simple pricing structure—small companies got 10 percent off the catalog price, medium-sized companies, 15 percent, and big companies, or whoever could talk me into it, got 20 percent. In a few years, my brother Harvey, who joined me a year and a half after I started, and I realized that this was a stupid idea, creating nothing but confusion for us. So we changed it to a straight 15 percent discount for everyone. That's another lesson for you. "Keep it simple." Don't overcomplicate things. I tried to follow that strategy throughout my business career. That's not to say you shouldn't embrace technology and new processes. We were, for example, one of the first mail order companies to install automated check readers so that every check that came in from a customer could be batched and automatically applied to the proper account and to the bank for deposit the same day, saving us a great deal of money and speeding up our deposits. I just mean that your strategies and your approach should be kept as simple as possible so you, and just as importantly, your people, understand them.

As one example, I remember, when the business was much bigger, one of our managers came to me saying they needed a new computer program in order to do a particular task. I asked how much the new program would cost us. Hundreds of thousands was the answer. I asked how much it would cost to hire more people to handle this particular task manually. I forget the exact answer, but it was a lot less than hundreds of thousands of dollars. So I told him to forget about the new, complex computer program and go hire more people. See, at the heart of the matter, business is simple.

We just let too many people (you and me included) complicate the heck out of it!

That first month in business, of cold-canvassing all over the city, plus calling on every friend I had who could help, I sold $960 worth of merchandise and made a $35 profit after gas and other expenses—not very much. By the time we sold the business, I figured out that we were doing that much volume about every 17 seconds!

There were a couple of things I did back then that, to this day, remain hallmarks of Quill. One is that I busted my back to give the best service possible. Whatever I sold one day I would call into the wholesaler the very next morning. Then, after spending the rest of the morning and a good part of the afternoon knocking on more doors, I would pick up that merchandise from the sales of the day before from the wholesaler and rush back to Dad's chicken store to pack the orders. I'd pile the packages in the trunk of my Ford and rush to the United Parcel depot by 6:30 P.M. so they would be on the last truck going out that day. Since all the business was in the Chicago area this guaranteed that if somebody ordered something on Monday, they would have it by Wednesday.

Each evening, my late wife Audrey would type up the invoices of shipments from that day so they could be mailed the next day and we could get our money as quickly as possible. (Incidentally, Audrey passed away from cancer four years before we sold the company.) Over the years, we got to the point that if someone ordered by 6 P.M., they would have their order the next day almost anywhere in the country and the invoices were sent the *following* day.

"Fanatical customer service"—I didn't invent that term, but we lived by it. No matter what kind of business you are in, you have a customer of some sort. If you don't figure out how to give the customer exactly what they need as quickly as possible (or even faster), somebody else will. And by the way, that fanatical customer service also applies to internal service, how everyone responds to the needs of other employees. That makes an amazing difference in how well your organization functions. You can't give your customers great service if you don't have great internal service throughout the company.

And through the years, we did just keep it simple: deeply discounted prices and great customer service on good quality merchandise.

The second thing I started doing back in 1956 that eventually defined Quill was direct mail. Within a few months of starting the business I sent out my first advertising piece. It was a penny postcard with five specials rather crudely handwritten on it. I mailed it to 160 people I had called on. Then, during the course of that first year, I followed that up with a series of black and white one-page mailings. I would just cut pictures out of the wholesaler's catalog, use a typewriter to set the copy, and penciled the headlines by hand. For some of the mailings I even included a free sample. Of course the samples were simply a rubberband or a strip of adding machine tape, and so on. Crude as they were, these mailings worked and convinced me that mailings were a valuable selling strategy.

By the end of that first year, I was making enough so that I could write checks for our household expenditures plus $15.00 per week to cover my expenses and then write a check from the company to cover those personal checks. That was a good thing, to say the least. Up until then, we were living completely off my wife's salary and our small savings account. And, as these things often go, two months after I started the business, she became pregnant with our first daughter. Eleven months after I started the business, I was a father. Talk about pressure to sink or swim! (More, by the way, later in this book on my philosophy about raising a family and growing a business at the same time. Believe me, it's not easy when you are putting in 60-to 70-hour weeks—which is often what it takes to start and establish a business.)

At about that same time, I was trying to convince my younger brother Harvey to join the business. It had been just a few years since he had gotten out of the Navy and he was now married with one child. Also having the entrepreneurial spirit, in September 1957 he quit his job working behind the counter at an electric supply company and joined me. We agreed we would each draw, $115 a week salary out of the business, meaning we had to get more business or lose money.

Now that Harvey was with me, doing all the office work from my home wouldn't work anymore. We needed a real office, which we couldn't afford. So we moved to a coal bin. That's right, a coal bin. My wife's Uncle Herb had a two-floor apartment building just a couple of blocks from the chicken store. He had converted from coal to oil heat and had this nice-sized unused coal bin in his basement. We figured it could make a perfect office. The rent was perfect, too—zero. There was just one thing standing in our way: a ton and a half of coal.

So Harvey and I spent a weekend—we would never miss a day of selling and processing orders—and shoveled that ton and a half of coal out of Uncle Herb's coal bin. We did it one wheelbarrow at a time. We'd shovel the coal up out the window, into a wheelbarrow, then into a truck we rented. From there, we hauled the coal to a dump. It took all weekend but we got it done. I remember Harvey and I returned to our homes and our wives wouldn't let us in—we were as caked with coal as miners. We had to strip in the hallway.

But we got that coal bin good and clean and painted it pink and blue. Yes, I know pink and blue aren't exactly the colors you might choose for an office. But just as cost savings would be a matter of life and death one day for Quill, we never spent money we didn't have to. And back then, it wasn't like we had a bunch to spend, anyhow. Harvey had blue paint left over at home from when he painted his son's nursery. I had pink paint left over from our daughter's nursery. And those became the colors for our first office.

The philosophy of never spending money we didn't need to spend stuck with us throughout our 43 years in business. I know too many people who start out their businesses with expensive furniture in overpriced offices. I'm not saying you need to operate out of a chicken store or a coal bin, but I am saying don't spend any dollar you don't absolutely need to. Oh, and by the way, our desks in that first office were old, enamel-topped, aluminum tubular-legged kitchen tables. I have always thought ours was the traditional way to start a business, except that we hadn't come over from the old country.

Anyhow, the business kept growing. We hired our first employee, a clerical assistant, because we were generating too many invoices for my wife to type up when she wasn't taking care of the children and the home. Fortunately, that first employee didn't mind walking through Uncle Herb's laundry hanging in the basement as she made it to our pink and blue office. Soon, we had to stock some items, for the first time having inventory. Since Uncle Herb and my father-in-law were brokers for hams we could get lots of wooden ham crates for free, which we nailed together into shelving. But it wasn't long before we outgrew the coal bin.

We moved a few blocks away into a storefront space and painted the windows black so that no one would think we were a retail store. We hired a bookkeeper and a full-time person to answer the phones.

We still had no formal business plan but, in our heads, we knew exactly where we were going—sort of. Our mailings continued to grow in size and number. They were also becoming more professional, using a freelance artist for good artwork and using a typesetter for real type. I still selected the products, designed the general themes and layout and wrote all the copy—usually in the evenings or on weekends. Soon, we were getting so many orders in response to the mailings that we had to spend more and more time inside taking orders. Finally, we found ourselves in the office all the time. We had just sort of slid into the mail order business. That had never been part of our planning. Originally, the mailings were just to support our outside sales efforts.


We became the first mail order office products dealer in the country. This led to our first business crisis, our first test of the determination and tenacious focus you need to make a business work. It turned out to be a much tougher test than shoveling one-and-a-half tons of coal.

Here's how it happened. We kept sending out mailings and, over time, they kept getting a little bigger, evolving from those penny postcards to 8-page, 12-page, 24-page, and then up to 64-page flyers. I was still working on them at night, and still writing the copy on an old manual typewriter. We started renting prospect names in addition to mailing to customers and other businesses we'd visited on our sales runs.

Our business was growing and we needed more space to stock items than we had in our 900-square-foot storefront space. So, proving that all things go full circle, we rented my dad's old chicken store. My father, unable to compete with the large grocery chain stores, had gone out of the retail business, becoming a chicken broker, selling chicken meat to manufacturers who used it in their products, such as frozen chicken pot pies. And this, happily, became a really good business for him—more profitable and much easier than the retail business.

Our sales flyers were now up to 64 pages but there was a real problem, one that cut into profits. Each year, we were still sending the full-line wholesaler's catalog to all of our customers. That meant it was sort of the luck of the draw whether we would get an order for something we stocked or an order for something we would have to get from the wholesaler. Not surprisingly, we made more money on a product we bought directly from the manufacturer and stocked. We realized that if we sold more of what we stocked, we could offer customers an even better discount and still make more profit. The margins were that much better if we sold what we got directly from the manufacturer than from the wholesaler.

So we decided to make the investments necessary to produce our own full-line catalog and to stock more items. The wholesaler would become a backup source for items the customer insisted on that we did not stock.

First, we rented the building next to Dad's old chicken store and broke through the walls, giving us the room necessary to stock more product. It was a chopped-up space with three retail store spaces plus a large first floor space and a basement reached by a stairway inside and a lift from the sidewalk outside. Not an ideal space, but inexpensive and roomy enough for our needs.

Second, we created our own full-blown catalog. I set up a separate office in the new part of the building, locking myself away with an assistant to produce the catalog. Leaving Harvey to run the business, I selected the items for our catalog, did rough layouts, wrote the copy, and worked with an art studio to produce a very professional-looking book. No more clipping pictures from the wholesaler's catalog and using a manual typewriter for type. It took nearly a year (1963) to produce this catalog.

To do all this, we used all the money we had accumulated plus $20,000 we had to borrow from the bank.

Then we mailed out the catalog and waited anxiously for the results.

Day after day, which became week after week, we waited for what we were sure was going to be an avalanche of new orders. At best, we got a ripple. Business was growing but perhaps at only a slightly better pace than before we sent out the catalog. And that wasn't good enough. Not with a few additional employees to pay who we had hired in anticipation of great results (a mistake and a lesson), more rent to pay, and a $20,000 note to pay down.

We didn't panic. Not at first. Then, after we had to let one employee go, we met on a weekend evening at Harvey's apartment with our father and my father-in-law. The agenda was what to do next. This was the sink or swim moment for Quill Office Products. My father and father-in-law urged us to get back out in the street and sell. We took a vote. The vote was three to one to hit the streets.

I was the one vote. I said no. I was firm in my belief that now that we were in it, mail order was the direction to go, that was what would make us different from our competitors. I also felt we could grow much bigger, expanding beyond the Chicago area, if we stuck with mail order, if we could make it work. I had started the business in a chicken store. As far as I was concerned, that gave me the right to be a dictator and ignore the vote. We continued with the mail order business and did not go back to the street.

After about five months, the orders finally began flowing in. The catalog was working. We learned an important lesson from this—nearly everything in business takes longer than you expect. In fact, I suspect that a lot of people in business forget this, or never realized it in the first place, and often give up right on the eve of success.

We came very close to making that mistake. Had we, it would have meant that Quill Office Products, later renamed Quill Corporation, would have remained a small local dealer providing a decent living. And that wouldn't have been so bad. It's just that, by then, my dream had expanded.

We eventually paid off the bank loan and began to accumulate money, keeping our salaries at a basic subsistence level and plowing everything else back into the business for more advertising and inventory. Soon, we needed more space and bought our first building, a 27,000-square-foot office and warehouse building just a few blocks from Dad's old chicken store.

Incidentally, that first building put us into the real estate business. Our accountant insisted we buy it personally, not through the business. This was great advice. Today, after selling Quill, we have a small real estate business and have built and own an industrial park with almost a million square feet of space on land we had purchased around our Quill headquarters.

By this time we were mailing to all of our customers plus 10,000 new prospects nationwide each week. And every six months we were producing a new, full-line catalog. Business really took off.

Within 11 years we had to move again, this time buying three acres of land in a suburb north of Chicago and building a modern one-story building. It was beautiful. Still is. We owned that building and rented it out after we outgrew it just seven years after building it.

At about that time, my brother Arnold, a CPA, joined the firm. So our management team was complete: me in marketing, Harvey in operations, and Arnold in finance.

Very quickly, that new building was too small. Here's how that happened. We were sending mailings once every three months, but because of a two-year record increase in inflation in the late 1970s, we could no longer guarantee our prices for even three months because manufacturers kept raising their prices. We would frequently receive copies of their old price lists rubber-stamped for example, "All prices up 10%." In order to deal with this, we decided to mail our customers *every* month, guaranteeing prices for that month only. To our amazement, as a result of these more frequent mailings, our business grew by more than 90 percent a year for the next two years (of course, later, I claimed that the increases were due to our marketing genius).

We had additional land to build on, but the business was growing so fast, we didn't have time to plan the expansion. So we rented additional space in the industrial park we were in. When we were finally able to spend time planning, we were operating with offices in three buildings and inventory in four others. We knew we had to move again, and started searching for land where we could build the Quill campus. In 1980, we bought an old tree nursery of about 35 acres and began construction on a 110,000-square-foot-warehouse with an attached 50,000-square-foot-office building, which we moved into in 1982. As time went on, we added another 110,000 square feet of warehouse and 100,000 square feet of office space. But I can tell you that before we did that, we were so crammed that we didn't have room for one more person in the office or any more product in the warehouse. We couldn't keep enough inventory to service our customers well without using the wholesaler a lot more than we wanted to.

And this is a critical lesson. We never moved or expanded facilities until we absolutely, positively had to and then not until we knew that we had enough business to *more than* cover the added costs. We learned our lesson very painfully in 1963. Too often, companies expand because their projections show they will be able to cover the costs—and when they don't, they find themselves in trouble, often having to sell the business or go out of business.

We were growing at a steady clip, always in the double digits. It seemed that the sky was the limit. But then the sky almost fell on our heads when Tom Stemberg created the first office product superstore and others quickly followed. *Their basic model was low, low pricing, buying in huge volumes and forcing the manufacturers to give them low prices, rebates, advertising allowances, and more.*

Staples. Office Depot. Office Max. These were the names that shot fear through the souls of thousands of independent office products dealers. The superstores, because they bought product in such volume, could dictate much lower prices from manufacturers than other dealers could get. As a result, the superstores could sell at drastically discounted prices and still make a profit. Also they may have been operating at slimmer margins, but the large volume of product they were moving made up for it. There was no way that independent office products dealers could match them in price.

At first, many in our business tried to ignore the superstores. They thought they were out of their minds, that the superstores could never sell at such drastically discounted prices and make money. They wrongly believed that nobody could live on such slim margins. They convinced themselves that the superstores would fail. Some even tried to force manufacturers not to sell to the superstores. A few manufacturers actually tried to protect their dealers but with the huge orders the superstores were delivering, eventually all the manufacturers decided to sell to them, usually at more favorable prices.

Just because I enjoyed doing it, I used to write a newsletter that I would mail to all our manufacturers. It became fairly influential in our business. At the time the superstores began showing up in the late 1980s, I wrote that anybody who thought the way to deal with the superstores was to ignore them and wait for them to fail was just putting their head in the sand—and would get it chopped off while they weren't looking. The superstores were going to completely redefine our business, I wrote. Most office products dealers ignored my warning. Nearly all of them are out of business. Over 15,000 small, independent office products dealers went out of business as a result of this, and our industry changed from a highly fragmented, inefficient industry into a much more organized highly efficient one. The consumers were better served with lower prices and better service.

At one point, there were close to 30 superstore chains. The folks who started and ran these companies came from other discount retailing industries—the food industry, hardware, and others. They came into our $100-billion-plus industry with an approach that dictated low, low everyday prices with frequent loss leaders, backed by rapid expansion of stores and massive amounts of advertising. They were used to low margins and they were like sharks smelling blood in the water once they understood how sloppy and bloated and highly splintered our industry was.

At Quill, our response was to wait and watch and not to panic. We carefully watched as one after the other, most of the new superstores failed. In the end, three survived: Staples, Office Depot, and Office Max. They continued to grow and became more and more dominant in the industry. One interesting side note of all of this was that, as the first one in the industry to really promote discounted prices, we were always considered the dirty price cutter. But then the superstores won that title and everyone began discounting.

During this entire period, Quill continued to grow and to remain profitable. But then, in 1990, we decided it was time to react. We decided we had to slash prices to meet the superstores' prices. We had made our mark in the business by being the first discounter, but now we had to discount our prices even further. The battle lines were clear and they were drawn along price points.

At the beginning of 1991, halfway through our fiscal year, we gathered our troops—our employees. We told them we were cutting prices deeply on all products across the board, with a few exceptions. The result was that from February of that year until the end of our fiscal year in September, we didn't make one dime of profit. We did end up making a profit that fiscal year but it all came from the first half.

We also told our employees to slash costs. We were very clear: if we didn't figure out how to cut costs to compete with the superstores, Quill would not survive. Everybody was focused on cutting costs. We did promise that no one would lose their job! And we promised that, if in our cost-cutting drive, somebody's job was eliminated we would find them another job in the company. How else could you expect someone to suggest a better way of doing something that would eliminate their position? We just figured that our continued growth, pushed even higher (we hoped) by our new, lower prices would absorb these people.

We became as fanatical about cutting costs as we were about customer service. In one instance, somebody came up with the idea of using a different type of lightbulb in the exit signs because they would last longer and as a result we would not have to change the bulbs as often. This saved us $12,000 a year in maintenance costs. We went from using three trailer loads of packing "peanuts" a day to just one, saving another $200,000 per year by developing a system for predetermining the smallest size carton we could use on an order *before* it was picked. We also invested $1 million in a complete desktop publishing system that eliminated the need to outsource design work, saving close to $3 million per year.

Finally, one of the things we did was to look at the bread and butter of how we make money: direct mail. We examined our mailing strategy closely and found an unbelievable amount of fat. With four, five, and six mailings going out to our customers every month, we were showing the same merchandise in at least two or three of the mailings all the time. The incremental increase in business was great. Our buyers were scared stiff at the thought of giving it up. But we had to ask ourselves, What are we paying to deliver this incremental increase in business? It turned out to be too much. We were losing money on that incremental business.

Not only that, we were mailing everything to just about everyone on our list. We didn't put enough thought into selectively segmenting these mailings. When margins were fat we didn't notice—doesn't mean it didn't matter, just means we didn't notice. Well, margins weren't fat anymore, not since the superstores were putting locations all across the nation and making all consumers—including even large companies—more cost conscious.

So we started cutting the fat out of our mailings, reducing the number of mailings. We got rid of the "multimailers," mailers stuffed with special offers each printed on a separate piece of paper, which, by the way, our customers hated. And we started to fine-tune our mailings so that we were sending only to "high-return" customers for specific products. For example, we slashed our mailing promoting tax forms from 400,000 to 37,000 high potential customers and actually sold more! We hadn't realized that most companies didn't buy tax forms—their accountants did.

It was a huge gamble, slashing what we charged for products to the point where we made no money. But we felt it was the only chance we had. Obviously, thanks to our ability to cut costs, it worked. By the next year, we were once again making a profit.

A lesson we learned then and that I applied very successfully when I bought another, much smaller, mail order company when I retired, was that there is always a lot of waste. You should always question *everything* you are doing, challenging yourself and your people to find a better, less expensive way to do it.

But there was one rule in our price cutting that we always followed. That rule was that we would do nothing that would reduce the service we gave our customers. We also applied that rule to any other changes we made, including the introduction of new technology.

I hate those automated telephone answering systems where you go from one set of options to the next and then end up with the recording, "Our agents are all busy servicing other customers. Your business is important to us. . . . " Yeah, my business is important to them. If it was so important, they would have a much more user-friendly system, and they would have enough agents to handle all the calls on the first ring, which was a rule we had.

It was also during this time that we redoubled our focus on customer service, changing our shipping policy, for example, from shipping every order within 8 to 24 hours out the door to any order in by 4 P.M., shipped the *same* day. Then we found a way to turn this into any order in by 6:00 P.M. Chicago time would be *delivered* the next day. To guarantee next day delivery, we opened warehouses around the country. We did it so that we could always stay a step ahead of our competitors when it came to customer service.

The mantra, so to speak, that had always guided Quill expanded now: not only were we committed to doing things right and providing superservice to the customer, we were equally committed to keeping costs down so we could sell at lower and lower prices. It was an equation that worked.

And this equation became simply a way of life at Quill, as routine as breathing: we were always able to find a way to cut costs and, at the same time, improve services. In fact, we learned that changing things to cut costs often resulted in better ways to do things for customers.

The end result was that Quill was the number one mail order office products company in the country.

Of course, as you know, we eventually decided to sell Quill to one of those superstores.

So that's a bit of our story. There's more to it, like the time we went before the U.S. Supreme Court and won in what has become a landmark case on interstate taxation of mail order sales. As we talk more, I'll share some of these stories. But for now, let's move to the lessons learned or, as I think of it, the non Ivy League MBA approach to building a great business.

By the way, you note I just said, "as we talk more." I hope this not-too-long book comes across as a conversation not a textbook. I'm just like you. Yes, right now I have a lot more money, but that took me 43 years of hard work. What it didn't require was any special degree or some unusually high IQ. My brothers and I were not geniuses, believe me. And I don't believe that most successful entrepreneurs are geniuses. They are simply hard working and highly focused individuals who become very, very good in the area they have chosen.

When young people approach me and ask how to become successful, I tell them to pick a niche and to become the smartest, most knowledgeable person in that niche (very few of us are capable of being smart in many areas) and then to work *very* hard.

What I am is someone who became successful in one such niche, and I want to tell you what I've learned along the way. These are general rules that, I believe, apply to almost every business. And I guarantee you this: listen to what I have to say, the lessons I've learned, and you'll be a more successful business man or woman.

To summarize this first chapter, I'd like to share a quote by Buddha with you: "Your work is to discover your work and then with all your heart to give yourself to it."

# Chapter 2

# What It Takes to Be an Entrepreneur

"Are entrepreneurs born or are they made?" "What does it take to be an entrepreneur?" Whenever and wherever I speak, or whenever I am talking with young, want-to-be-entrepreneurs, I am asked these questions. I've even read articles on them.

One dictionary defines an entrepreneur as "A person who organizes, operates, and assumes the risk for business ventures." Another states, "A person who undertakes an enterprise or business with the chance of profit or loss." Both definitions say that, first, an entrepreneur is a person who is willing to take the gamble and second, that they have the desire to start and run a company knowing that it is possible the company may fail. They are betting on their own ability—and are willing to bet a lot on that ability.

As to the question of whether entrepreneurs are born or made—I come down on the side that they are born. But a lot can happen in life that does help to make an entrepreneur, or at least to open a door for him or her and to help make them better. Yes, there is a lot that can be learned about how to be a better entrepreneur, about how to run a good business. In fact, this kind of learning is an endeavor that lasts one's entire business life. You don't just get it from schools. In fact, most of it you learn as you go along. Hopefully, you learn from your mistakes, and there will be plenty of them. You learn by talking to your vendors, by going to trade shows and seminars. You learn by talking with other entrepreneurs. You learn from people you hire who are smarter than you or who have had different experiences. And you learn from reading trade journals and general business publications and books.

There is no end to how much and from whom you can learn. But that's only possible if you are constantly trying to learn. Why do so many entrepreneurs read, for example, *BusinessWeek?* Because they are constantly trying to learn (put another way, they are constantly trying to steal an idea or two). And if you want to be a *very* successful entrepreneur you must always be learning. Your goal must be to become one of the experts in your specific field as well as to build a wealth of general business knowledge. Clients and customers need to know that they can call you for advice and that it will be worth something. That it is rare in the marketplace.

But I'm going to be blunt. You can study and learn until your business IQ is Einsteinlike, but if you don't have "it"—if you weren't born with something in your being that makes a great entrepreneur—you're not going to be the entrepreneurial type. There simply has to be something in your makeup that lets you take risks and chafes at the idea of working for others all your life.

In the first place, you must have confidence in yourself and in your own abilities. And you must be a believer in the free enterprise system, the system that gives you a chance to succeed or fail, based on your own talents, your own drive, your own persistence. Sadly, too many Americans see excuses in the free enterprise system. "You can't make it today, not like the old days. Today the entire marketplace is controlled by venture capitalists and big business." I don't care how crowded the field is, there is always room for someone with a better idea or maybe for someone with an old idea but who is willing to work hard to do a better job at it. An entrepreneur understands this for what it is: opportunity. Opportunity to take a chance, to succeed perhaps beyond your dreams, or to fail.

In my own case, it was almost preordained that I was going to be an entrepreneur. I wasn't a joiner. I lasted in the Boy Scouts for about a year, in a college fraternity for one school year, in the National Guard for the minimum amount of time. I just wasn't happy being part of an organization and being told what to do. In the sports area, I was interested only in individual sports, weight lifting and gymnastics.

In my work experience, not counting working my way through college and earlier experiences, I was pretty much on my own. My first real job after college was as a travelling salesman for a food company. I would pack the trunk of my car with samples and would be on the road, by myself, for four to five weeks, and then in the office for a few days or a week and then back on the road again. Whether I was born with it or picked it up along the way, I was destined to do my own thing. It has been that way all my life. I guess that's why I always like that old song Frank Sinatra used to sing, "My Way." And I certainly would not fit into a large organization with all the bureaucracy and slow, group decision making. (Ross Perot, founder of Electronic Data Systems [EDS] once put it nicely when he said, "When you see a snake, you kill a snake. You don't form a committee to decide what to do about it.")

Successful entrepreneurs make decisions. You have to be that kind of person to be a successful entrepreneur, and I don't think that is something that is learned. It's a part of who you are. Indeed, I would venture to say that I can spend a day with somebody at his workplace, watching and listening to him work, and by the end of the day tell you whether he could make it as an entrepreneur. The key? Decision making—the ability and willingness to make decisions. Even a bad decision leads to action that, if the decision turns out badly, can lead to feedback and correction. A decision may lead to just doing things as they have been done which, by the way, is not always a bad thing. If the way they have been done is truly the best way they can be done.

You don't have to be a wild risk taker. In fact, most entrepreneurs I know are fairly cautious sorts. They made the big gamble when they went into business for themselves. And they may take other big gambles when the circumstances demand it. But by and large, they are averse to taking undue risks and possibly endangering the company. But on the other hand, they are not the type of people who need to be 120 percent sure that something will work before they try it. Being 60 percent sure is good enough for most entrepreneurs. Then they depend on their abilities and experience to carry them the other 40 percent. (Of course, if you have built up some cash reserves, that also helps.) By not betting the whole ranch on any one endeavor and by going with what their gut tells them (based on their own experience), along with their confidence that they can shape results, is enough for them.

Obviously, not all entrepreneurs are alike. Some are huge risk takers and love betting the ranch, and they often go bust several times during their careers. You see this a lot in real estate developers. And, of course, not all are the go-it-alone type of personality that I always was. Many entrepreneurs love team sports and fraternity life. There is an amazing variety of successful entrepreneurs. Introverts and extroverts. People with MBAs and others without any college education. Or as my wife would probably put it, "Tall, short, thin, fat, and everything in between."

Especially these days, entrepreneurs come in all colors, all ethnicities, genders, religions, and countries of origin. In fact, that's one of the great things about our country. It was founded on the principle that everyone had a chance to make it for themselves. Capitalism was always a basis for our economy. And that opened the door for everyone. Also there were no kings or queens or princes and princesses.

So I've talked about what has to be in you to make you an entrepreneur. Now let me talk about what I believe you must do to be a successful one. It comes down to two words: "work hard." I know a handful of people who seem to be successful entrepreneurs without working hard. But they are few and far between, and in most of the cases I know of, these people are working with (a lot of) family money. But for just about everyone else who wants to be a successful entrepreneur it's going to take a heck of a lot of plain old hard work. Very hard. Very long hours. And that cuts the potential competition down a lot.

These days I hear a lot about living a "balanced" life. I suppose that means being able to do everything: work, spend time with family, take time to be with the kids a lot, and to indulge in hobbies or personal, favorite activities. In other words, it means getting to do it all. But from my experience and my observations, successful entrepreneurs don't get to do all of that. The business just takes up too much of their time. Heck, I didn't even take up golf until I was sixty-eight years old. It just takes up too many hours. An hour on the handball court did me just fine. (And, of course, my 6:00 A.M. workouts with the weights, which was and is a lifelong endeavor.)

These days, you read all kinds of newspaper articles about how Americans work too hard, putting in so many hours, many more than Europeans do. The writers of these articles seem to feel that a 30- or 35-hour work week, four weeks of vacation, holidays, plus plenty of time off to attend to family matters should be the norm. For the average working person, they're wrong. (Just compare the economics.) And for the entrepreneur that schedule is beyond totally unrealistic.

If you are going to build a successful business, 60- to 70-hour weeks would more nearly be the norm. And, in the beginning, at least, there may be no vacations. I went about six years after starting my business before taking a vacation. And it wasn't until a few years before we sold—in other words for 39 years—that I went to the office every Saturday for half a day, at least. The other five days were 7:30 A.M. until at least 6:00 P.M., and I often took work to do at home.

Obviously, you have to be a self-starter to be an entrepreneur because there's no one above you to get you started. But what you don't have to be is good at everything. No one is. But if you are smart, you begin surrounding yourself with people who are much better than you are in places where you are weak. I have known successful entrepreneurs who were great at sales but terrible in administration. Some who were great with people and others who were terrible with them.

Many successful entrepreneurs have partners who are good where they are weak. The usual combination is the Mr. Outside and the Mr. Inside. In my own case, I was lucky that my brother Harvey joined me about a year and a half after I started because he was a great operations guy with a terrific eye for details. I was more focused on marketing, merchandising, and advertising. When we got to be about three-and-a-half million in size, our other brother, Arnold, who was a CPA, joined us and handled all the financial matters, the bookkeeping and collections as well as personnel.

What a great team we made, the kind of team every entrepreneur has to build if he or she really wants to grow the company. No one has all the knowledge and talent to do it all. But the key is to surround yourself with very talented people. Don't be afraid to hire people who are as smart and talented as you are, or even more so.

I put in tons of hours working to build Quill. But I never felt like I was missing out on life. To a great extent during those years, my life was my business. I doubt that a great pianist like Mozart ever feels he's putting in too much time honing his craft. And, to me, that's what business is: a craft. And I certainly enjoyed the endless pursuit of honing my craft.

If you asked me whether it was worth it, my answer would be an unqualified, "Yes!" Starting and building a successful company was one of the most exciting, most satisfying experiences I have ever had. Pablo Picasso, Rembrandt, Jascha Heifetz, Harry Houdini, and all the other great artists of whatever medium all probably felt the same way about their careers in their chosen fields. For me, business was the best game in town. It became a part of the seamless fabric of my whole life.

# Chapter 3

# Getting Started

When I speak to college classes or to other would-be entrepreneurs, one of the questions I am asked most often is, "How do I get started?" The answer usually breaks down into a number of parts, including what kind of business to go into, how to get financing, how much risk one is comfortable with, and more. In this chapter, I give you some things to think about in terms of getting started.

The first thing I tell would-be entrepreneurs is that this is probably one of the best and the easiest times to start a business that I have seen. That's because in a great many cases the quality of customer service is probably at the lowest level I have ever seen since I started Quill in 1956. Create a business where one of your basic values is really relating to a human being, and you are golden.

Great customer service, as someone once said, does not cost. It makes a profit. Unlike at Quill, today when there is a choice to be made between saving some money or providing great customer service, the MBA types in big companies almost always choose saving the money.

That leaves a great big open door for an aggressive, customer service-oriented entrepreneur. So when you are thinking of getting started, don't let the fact that there are some big companies in the industry scare you off. I guarantee you, there is an unserved or underserved niche there, which is another thing you should think about: the idea of finding a niche in which you can become better than anyone else.

My experience and observation tells me that most people go into a business with which they have had some relationship and familiarity. Their parents or other family members were in the business and they had some exposure to it, or they worked for a firm in that business. Or maybe they had a hobby or a special interest that led them into the business they chose. In my own case, as you read, I got into the office supply business because I had been a partner in a firm selling briefcases to businesses in Chicago and wanted more product to carry when I went out on my own. Office supplies seemed a natural line to add. My years of experience in the food industry calling on distributors across the country gave me a good insight into the distribution industry, even if in an unrelated field.

Of all the businesspeople I know, no one simply did a study and chose an industry and a product line with which they had no previous connection. I am sure that such people do exist, but they are certainly a minority. So if you want to start a business, my suggestion is to look to your own experiences and see how they and your natural ability can best be put to use. Or you could do a study of fields that look promising and then go to work for a firm in that field before you branch out on your own.

You don't want to open up your shop blind, so to speak. There are a few things you might want to look at before jumping in. How big is the total field? If it's a very small industry, you may never get the chance to grow big. On the other hand, it could be a small field where you can fill a niche and do quite well. I know one man who has a company that makes small brushes for electric motors. This is such a small field that no large manufacturer wants to get into it, and he is almost alone in supplying the brushes. That's a nice position to be in and he does quite well. But there aren't many like that.

On the other hand, there are many fields that are quite big, where you can pick a small niche and become the leading expert in that niche. And you also have the possibility of growing beyond that niche and becoming quite large. In the office products industry, we grew to over $630 million and still had only a small percentage of the total field. Staples, Office Depot, and Office Max were doing as much as from $3 to $10 billion each, and that was still just a small percentage of what has grown to be a several hundred billion dollar market.

That is something I often tell young people. None of us are geniuses, I tell them. But each of us can choose a small niche and become the leading expert in that niche. I have a friend in the fruit business. But he doesn't carry all kinds of fruit. He specializes in mangoes. I had never even heard of mangoes before I met him. But he has made himself an expert in everything relating to that one fruit, has found the best sources for them, and became the supplier of mangoes to all the major food chains in the Chicago area. He makes a good living at it.

Another friend is in the insurance business. He evolved from just selling insurance, where he got his first experience into specializing only in life insurance as a vehicle for estate planning and investment. He deals almost exclusively with successful business owners. And while other insurance people I know claim to know this end of the business, this friend has made a real study of it, has made the right connections with the right insurers, and is truly an expert in the field. Yes, he does very well.

In today's business world, it's probably fair to say that the most valuable commodity is knowledge. If you have either unique knowledge or deeper knowledge than your competitors, you will be in demand—you will be able to sell. That's my point here—whatever field you choose, pick one segment of it and work hard to become a real expert in that segment.

In our case, we originated the mail order segment of the office products industry. We worked at it and learned all we could about mail order marketing and distribution. We joined the Direct Marketing Association, went to seminars, read books and magazines, and even made it a point to seek out and talk with some of the top people in the field of direct marketing. While most of the 15,000 office products dealers sold through outside salespeople or through retail stores, we sold by direct marketing. A few others, but not many, followed our lead.

Here's another question to ask yourself: is it a field or a type of business suited to your talents and temperament? Being an entrepreneur is very demanding in time and effort. So you had better like what you will be doing. Most successful entrepreneurs really do love their businesses. It becomes a very important part of their lives. It often dominates family conversations, and many social events and friendships usually develop from it. You better be willing to put in long hours. And who wants to, in fact who can, put long hours into something they don't love doing? No one who wants to be happy and stay sane and stick to it for any long period of time, that's for sure.

Then, ask yourself about financing. Most new entrepreneurs will not be going into highly capital-intensive businesses, such as manufacturing cars or trailer homes and so on. For those who will be going into such businesses, the question of financing is far beyond the scope of this book. Besides, those folks are very experienced and know how to go about getting the financing they need.

However, most would-be entrepreneurs are thinking on a much smaller scale, with much more modest goals. In my own case, I started with just the idea of wanting to make a good living. It was many years before I realized that we had the potential for much more. Does the acorn dream of becoming a mighty oak? Maybe. But what happens to the acorn is akin to what happens with start-up businesses. Some make it. Some don't.

Almost all the major companies in the United States including firms such as Ford, Dell, Subway, and Crate and Barrel started on a shoestring as small ventures with capital supplied by the entrepreneur from his savings or from borrowings from family and friends. And that's not a bad way. In fact it's probably a very good way to start.

Of course, today there is a whole pot full of private equity funding available. There are thousands of individuals and partnerships looking for opportunities to invest in private firms. If there is no other way to get financing, this may be a way to do it. The risk is spread and doesn't rest solely on the entrepreneur. (But, of course, if you are risk averse, you probably wouldn't be comfortable as an entrepreneur, anyhow.) Another advantage is that you can be better financed and therefore get a faster start and grow faster. This is the kind of money that fueled the dot-com craze that eventually flamed out in 2000.

However, the downside of this is that it may take you years to develop a good business plan and to shop that plan to startup venture capitalists. They are besieged by people who want to start businesses and they sift through hundreds of requests for the one or two that they might be interested in investing in. If you find one to invest in your venture, then you have a partner who wields a lot of power and whose goal is usually to sell the business in a few years and walk away with a nice profit for his investors. Besides there are very few venture capital firms that want to invest in an untested individual with just a business plan.

Most venture capital firms realize that the vast majority of the plans overstate sales and profit expectations and underestimate potential problems. In other words, most projections don't meet expectations. So whether you go to a venture capital firm (or individual) or whether you start on a shoestring, my advice is that you should never believe your own projections. You can hope that they are right, but don't spend money in anticipation that the projected results will materialize as projected. They usually won't. Even when you are well on your way, you shouldn't invest, or "bet on the come," unless you have the resources to pay for the shortfall if it occurs. If you do, you can find yourself in deep trouble.

I believe that there is a basic decision to be made when thinking of financing your startup venture as well as financing it later on. That question, simply put, is how independent, how much in charge of your own destiny do you want to be?

The old saying, "He who pays the piper calls the tune," is very true when you use outside investors to finance your startup or fuel your growth. Investors, naturally, want a return on their investment and an exit strategy. This can put a major crimp into running the business the way you want to, especially as a family business. At some point you may have to go public or even sell the business when you would rather keep it as a privately held business.

Financing the startup from your own savings or from family money and starting with the office in your home or some low-cost location may mean a slower startup and slower growth, but it has the advantage of giving you (and your partner if you have one) 100 percent control over the business. There is a lot to be said for that.

Of course, there are other ways of going into business. You might buy a business from someone who is retiring or wants out for some other reason. Or, if you are lucky enough to be a part of a family in business, you might start up as an offshoot of that business, assuming you don't want to just join the family business. There are endless permutations on these themes.

From the time I started the business until the day we sold it, as I mentioned earlier, we provided the bank with our financials every single month. We actually borrowed money for the business only three times, way back at the beginning: Once we borrowed just to show our IT people the cost of buying a new piece of equipment. But keeping the bank informed did help us out tremendously in various real estate ventures (all of them at first related to the business and then, after we sold the business, some that were pure real estate deals). We had, over the years, built up such a good rapport with our banker that it made it very easy to do some great things with real estate because he knew us and trusted us. And if from time to time you need money to help you grow or to carry you over some seasonal needs, and so on, that kind of relationship is invaluable. I believe it most easily comes when your banker has had a long, close relationship with you.

I talked about great oaks growing from little acorns. Perhaps another way of making the point is that old Chinese saying, "A tree that reaches past your embrace grows from one small seed. A structure over nine stories begins with a handful of earth. A journey of a thousand miles starts with a single step." (Tao).

Finally, the most important piece of advice I can give you about getting started is that while you may have a destination in mind, it is critical that you enjoy the journey. You may never reach your visualized destination, but you can have a good time along the way—and make a very good living. If you do reach that dreamed-of destination and find the pot of gold at the end, all the better.

# Chapter 4

# Financing

In financing a business, from startup all the way through the life of the business, some basic questions need to be answered and then some strategies to be considered. The questions relate to your own individual and personal preferences, while the strategies apply to all businesses.

The first question you have to ask yourself is: Would I rather own 100 percent of a smaller entity or a much smaller, and perhaps not even controlling percentage, of a large entity? As I have said, when I started Quill, I started with $2,000 from my father-in-law and enough in the bank to live on for a little while. Plus my wife was working. I owned Quill 100 percent. When my brother Harvey joined me a year and a half later, he put in about $2,500 for his share. Then, 25 years later, our brother Arnold joined. We never sought outside money and were never interested in going public (which was probably one of the best decisions we ever made).

Another approach is to find working partners who can put up some money so your pool of cash is bigger and your ownership share is still large. This, of course, is what happened when my brother Harvey joined me, although $2,500 was not exactly a huge infusion of cash. When looking for an outside working partner, you would probably be looking for a lot more since you already started the business.

A third way, which I have already mentioned and today a very popular way, is to start with venture capital. The entrepreneurs starting and running the business have only a portion of the stock and are answerable to the investors, who are interested only in getting a good return on their investment, usually within five years, which in their eyes is a long-term investment. A lot of individuals have been very successful with this kind of start-up. (As a side note, I have invested in a start-up company and have attended board meetings, and if I ever hear the term "burn rate" again, I will know to head for the exits. It's a term that means how fast we are "burning" money. In other words, there are no profits and we are spending a lot of money).

Of course, how you finance your business depends a great deal on the type of business you want to have. Some businesses require a great deal of equipment and space to get started. Others you can literally start in your basement and require little investment. Once your business is up and running there are other, more controllable, factors that dictate your need for outside money, and that is where the question of strategies comes in.

My own, very strong preference is to own and control what I spend my life building. I would prefer to have 100 percent of a much smaller entity than a much smaller percent of a much bigger entity. I guess I like the sentiment in those lines from "Invictus," "I am the master of my fate; I am the captain of my soul." I prefer to be the master of my fate, totally responsible for what I do, for what I achieve.

In my opinion, whichever way you start, once started, it is critical to try to run as debt free as possible. (Many people don't agree with me on this, preferring using debt to grow faster.) But believe me, it can be done, even at a very large company. The last time we borrowed money (except for the aforementioned time, when we borrowed just to show IT the cost of capital) was in 1963. From then on, when we were doing far less than $1 million in volume, until we sold the business in 1998, when we were doing more than $630,000,000 in volume, we never again borrowed for the business. We grew it entirely out of retained earnings. That is where the strategic choices come in.

One of the most important choices is deciding what you want to do with profits once you begin making them. Do you leave them in the business to fuel future growth or take them out to lead a better life or to invest in the stock market or elsewhere? Many entrepreneurs, once they begin to make money in their business join country clubs, upgrade their houses, their cars, their whole style of living. In moderation, this is certainly not a bad thing to do—many entrepreneurs have put off many of these things during the years it took to become profitable. But when done to the point where it drains the business of too much of the money that could be used for growth, it is a stupid thing to do.

Throughout our entire careers at Quill, my brothers and I preferred to plow back most of the earnings into the company. We paid ourselves fair but modest salaries and our bonuses were based on the same criteria as everyone else's. Even after we were generating more cash than needed for growth, we put aside a great deal in bonds to make sure we had enough in case we hit some rough times in the business. I guess we believed in the biblical story of the pharaoh's dream about the seven fat cows followed by the seven thin cows. Joseph interpreted this for him to mean that seven good years of harvest would be followed by seven years of drought and poor harvest. He counseled the pharaoh to save something from the seven good years to hold the people over during the seven bad ones.

I still believe in that concept. Things will not always be good. It is important to have plans and provisions for when you hit some rough spots. I know that in today's world of instant gratification that this is a difficult concept to accept, but it is important. People who are highly leveraged in their business (and this applies to their private lives as well) are always in danger of losing everything when things turn rough, as they inevitably always do at some point.

Then there are those who take money out of their business to invest in the stock market or elsewhere instead of investing it in their own business. In my opinion, as well as in the opinion of many other knowledgeable people, you cannot make more money investing somewhere else than you can investing in your own business. That is, of course, if you have a decent business and if you have faith in yourself. A friend of mine, who took over his father-in-law's business, used to spend a great deal of his time investing a lot of money in the stock market. He thought I was foolish for not doing so. His business went bankrupt. We sold ours for a great deal of money, which in the end was the greatest equity deal possible. The lesson is, focus on your own business and invest in your own business.

So, living *relatively* modestly and retaining a good deal of the profits in the business is one way of financing the business and its growth. Another way, and one that is very rich in potential for most businesses, is by improving the cash flow, focusing on such things as inventory management, accounts receivable, and accounts payable. Handled badly, they are a major drain on cash. Handled well, they improve the cash flow quite a bit. Handled brilliantly, they can provide an amazing amount of cash.

If you have a million dollar inventory and turn it six times a year instead of three, you free up $500,000 worth of cash. For each inventory turn improvement after that, you free up another $100,000. It is not that difficult to improve inventory turns. It simply requires a great deal of attention and better negotiations with vendors. Don't load up on new items until they become proven sellers. Negotiate to get the bigger discounts based on yearly volume instead of the size of each order. The whole world is getting used to just-in-time inventory management and the trucking industry is sophisticated enough these days to be a good partner in this. Get rid of unsaleable merchandise somehow, at some price.

Reducing receivables also puts a lot of cash into your business. If your terms are net 30 days, then you should be shooting for receivables in the 35- to 40-day range. There will always be some slow paying accounts. But to have receivables in the 45-, 50-, or 60-day range is unacceptable and is draining money from your operation. Again, to simplify things, let's assume that you are doing $12 million a year, $1 million a month. Thirty-day receivables would therefore mean one million dollars in accounts receivable. So each additional day of receivables would mean another $33,333.00 tied up in receivables. So if you are at 40 days, that is $333,333.00. At 50 days, $666,666.00, and so on.

Improving your collection time is critical. We found a simple methodology that we used almost from the beginning and never changed—because it worked. First, invoices were sent out the day following shipment. Always! We have seen many firms that didn't send invoices until two, three, and even five or six days after shipment. This just extended the collection period from the date of shipment.

Next, five days following our net 30-day terms, we sent a follow-up, a reminder notice, nicely worded. Fifteen days after that, if the invoice was still unpaid, we sent a stronger reminder. Fifteen days later, they would get a still stronger letter, or, if the size of the invoice warranted it, a phone call. By this time, it is very important to make sure that there was no problem, such as an unresolved damage claim, that was holding up payment. But if there was no such problem, it was soon after that we turned the receivable over to a collection agency. We knew that the longer a bill remained unpaid, the more likely it was to turn into a bad debt, and we wanted to keep our bad debts down to a minimum.

Another thing we did was to create a credit status for each customer, which would tell us how much open credit, if any, we should give to each customer based on their payment history. We were not hesitant to put certain accounts on a COD or even a cash-in-advance basis. Also, we created special maximum credit limits for new accounts based on their industry and their size.

As we grew, we became better and better at each of our credit functions, but the basic formula never changed—because it worked.

A word of warning: when you are dealing with someone's credit standing, you are dealing with their reputation, a very delicate subject. Be firm, but always be careful, courteous, and pleasant.

Also examine your payment terms. For many years, our terms were 1 percent 10, net 30 days—meaning that the customer got 1 percent off their bill if they paid within 10 days. But after we began to have enough money in the business, we figured out that paying 1 percent to collect our money 20 days earlier was like paying 18.25 percent interest since there are 18.25 20-day periods in the year. Actually it was like paying even more because many people took the 1 percent even when they paid in 15 or 20 days. So we discontinued the 1 percent 10-day terms and although our receivables, of course, slowed down a bit, our bottom line benefited.

The flip side of collections is payables. You want to collect your receivables as quickly as possible, but the longer you can stretch out your payables, the more money you have to grow your business. I am not suggesting that you simply pay your bills late. But I am suggesting that you negotiate better payment terms. You might be surprised what you can negotiate. The big guys do it all the time. Maybe you can get a better discount for fast payment, or, if you are awash in cash, for prepayment. Or maybe you can negotiate 45-day or even 60-day terms. They are there to be had. But whatever you negotiate, stick to those terms. Keep your word and pay on time, as negotiated.

Finally, another source for cash is found by cutting waste. *Every* business has waste, often lots of it. Many businesses are like a leaky pail where a lot of the water you put in simply leaks away. For more on this, refer to the chapter "You Can, Too, Argue with Success!"

Now, I said I don't like debt. But it is still very important to have a good relationship with your bank because, if all of the above are not sufficient, the bank is, of course, a good source of funds. I've detailed how to build such a relationship in the chapter "About Advisors and Boards."

As I have in other places in this book, I want to emphasize that it's not genius that accomplishes all this. It is simply an unrelenting focus on making it happen and lots of hard work.

Simply keep in mind, throughout the course of growing and building your business, one of the most critical elements in building and maintaining a successful business is cash management. The health and future of your business is determined by thoughtfully deciding how much you leave in the business; the management of inventories, receivables, and payables; and the vigor of cost savings efforts. Cash permits life sustaining and enhancing activities for your company such as more marketing efforts, the hiring of good personnel, purchasing merchandise on better terms, and much more. It also helps cover the inevitable waste (which is *always* there no matter how much of it you eliminate), the programs that don't work, the errors in hiring, the goods that can't be sold, and so on.

Make no mistake about it. A good cash flow in a business is just as essential as is good blood circulation to your body.

## Chapter 5

# The Miracle of Hard Work

You read a lot in the papers these days about "leading a balanced life," about the fact that Americans work so much harder than Europeans, and that we should cut down on the amount of work we do. You also hear a lot about being "burned out." (Although in some cases I often wonder how some people can be burned out when they were never lit in the first place.)

Well, here's a simple test to determine if you can be a successful entrepreneur:

| | | |
|---|---|---|
| Do you think we should be working hours more like the Europeans, as little as 35 hours a week and as much as one month vacation a year? | ☐ Yes | ☐ No |
| Is your primary goal a "balanced life?" | ☐ Yes | ☐ No |
| Does getting burned out worry you? | ☐ Yes | ☐ No |

If you answered yes to any of these questions, then I would say the odds of your becoming a successful entrepreneur are not great. You might do better taking all of your money to Vegas.

I know a lot of very successful entrepreneurs and I don't know a single one of them who leads what most people would call a balanced life, who worked anywhere near what would, even in this country, be called "normal" hours, and who was ever burned out. Although some successful entrepreneurs do feel burned out after 30 or 40 years of building their business, others can go on until they die.

Yet most of them have had very good families and have very good kids. (My theory on that is because most of them are good

47

role models—they are responsible, work hard, and aren't spending time on wasteful, if not harmful, activities, like hanging at the bar, gambling, or philandering.) All through their careers there was never even the thought of being burned out. In fact they are some of the most energetic people I know. They loved what they were doing and the more they did of it, the more energized they became. And they had a lot of fun along the way. Maybe it wasn't the kind of fun some people envision, but it was for that kind of person.

If you come into this worried about a balanced life, worried about how many hours you will put in at the office, the plant, or the shop, worried about getting burned out, you shouldn't think about being an entrepreneur. You should get a 9 to 5 job somewhere, not expect to rise too high in the company, and be happy to live on whatever the job pays. And there's nothing wrong with that—unless you want to be really successful.

I think Pat Ryan, founder and chairman of AON Corporation, one of the world's largest insurance firms, with revenues well into the billions, said it very well one time when he was interviewed for a newspaper article. "I think the price is commitment. A lot of people don't get committed and don't stay with it. I think the price is hard work." He went on to say, "I think the price is striking the right balance in your life, but knowing that if you're going to succeed professionally, you've got to spend an inordinate amount of time doing that."

"Very few people," he continued, "who have been successful have been able to do it without a tremendous time commitment. And a lot of those who didn't take a lot of time to make it, also didn't keep up." That, in my opinion, says it all.

That was exactly the philosophy we had. The price we paid for success was to have a tremendous focus on the business. That included 10- and 12-hour days during the week and lots of work on weekends. Almost right up until we sold the company, after 43 years, I was still working those kinds of hours, still getting into the office by 7:30 A.M. and staying until about 6:00 P.M. and coming in for half a day or more on Saturdays. About five years before we sold the business, we began taking Saturdays off and what I thought would happen did happen.

When we were working Saturdays, many of our managers, buyers, and others also showed up. But one Saturday after we had quit coming in on Saturdays, I had to pick up something from my office. You could have blown a cannon off in the place and not hit anyone. So I guess you can say that what the leader does has a multiplying effect, good or bad.

While we were living the kind of commitment Ryan spoke of, we didn't ignore our families, not in the least. Was there a lot of time for our families? There was always enough time. When Harvey and I set up our first office in Uncle Herb's coal bin in Chicago, we decided that the wives wouldn't care what time we started in the morning but they would care what time we got home at night. So we often left our homes around 6:30 A.M. so we could be in the office by 7:30 or before. And we wound our day up by about 6:00 P.M. so we could be home for dinner and have some time with our wives and kids. Of course, we often took reading or work home for after the kids went to bed. Saturday afternoons and Sundays were for the family, although, as I mentioned, we often squeezed in a little work then also.

There's no question that my late wife, Audrey, shouldered most of the burden of raising the kids, shopping, preparing meals, taking care of the house, and so on. She saw that as her job. My job was to build the business and make a living. My daughter Judy was on the school gymnastic team and I never missed one of her meets. Whenever they were on a weekday, I did take off a few hours to make sure I was there.

But I never took off to play golf, something that takes a good part of a day. I finally did take it up when I was about sixty-eight and I joined a country club. I am still forever amazed when, during the week, I see young guys out there, not even with customers, playing golf. It's hard for me to imagine that there is not business to be tended to. That's my point. There is *always* business to be tended to. Successful entrepreneurs not only accept this, they embrace it. And they build real balance, infused by the commitment Ryan talked about. Yes, they usually have wonderful relationships with their children, but they also work at home after their children go to sleep. They work some on weekends when their children are off doing something else. They even often take a bit of work with them on vacation. And they don't get burned out by this, they get energized by it!

I'm not saying that someone cannot make a decent living and cannot achieve modest success as an entrepreneur without focusing so intensely on the business. There are many folks who have decent small-sized or maybe even mid-sized businesses and do fairly well financially. And that is fine if that is what you want.

But if you truly want to have a great company, be a big success, then there is a price to pay. And part of that price is that you have to work very hard at it. On the other hand, there is a huge reward also, and I don't mean just a financial reward. There is the reward of achieving the best you are capable of achieving, the deep down satisfaction of being the best you are capable of being. And by doing that you provide your family, your kids, with something invaluable: a great role model.

Also, by building a great business, you have added a good deal to the world. You have serviced a need better than someone else. You've employed a good many people and have been able to provide them with steady jobs at good pay so they could raise their families well. So many people pay lip service—sometimes unending lip service—to making a contribution to the world. But few people make as big a contribution as do businesspeople. And the people who bad-mouth business and who talk and talk and talk about "doing something good for the world instead" just don't understand how the world works. Medical research, education, public works, and just about everything else we can think of gets done only if it is funded. And that funding comes from willing individual donors or from money that the government has taken from not-so-willing taxpayers. But either way, it comes from the result of what businesses do. Money does not just, as the old saying goes "grow on trees."

Do people work hard to become doctors or lawyers or other types of professionals? Sure they do, and they deserve a lot of credit for it. But entrepreneurs work just as hard, or harder, and spend probably more years not making a great living, before they are successful.

I look back at what we did with Quill, from a phone in my dad's chicken store to a more than $630-million-a-year business, and I realize it's a miracle. It's the miracle of hard work. Don't think you can't do the same thing. You can. Combine your dreams and your ambitions with unremitting hard work, and there's a good chance you will achieve your own miracle.

## Chapter 6

# The Magic of a Vision

A quote I like a good bit is "It is difficult to make predictions—especially about the future." Every day, in newspapers, on radio, on television, pundits are predicting the future with great certainty. Follow up on those predictions later, and the only thing certain is that the vast majority of the time they were wrong.

The most famous of them is the Malthusian theory, put forth in the *Essay on the Principle of Population* in 1799. Thomas Malthus predicted that if the world population continued to grow at the rate that it was then growing, there wouldn't be enough food to feed everyone and the result would be mass starvation. Today, 207 years later the world's population is six-and-a-half times larger and the world has an overproduction of food, with new and better ways of producing food being constantly discovered.

In reality, there's only one way to predict the future with any degree of accuracy. Actually, it's not predicting the future, it's shaping the future. You can shape the future. You can envision what your life and business should look like 1, 5, 10, 20 years down the road, and you can work hard to make it happen. That's what I mean by the Magic of a Vision. A vision is what drives your every action, and with the right vision, strongly held, it's what can drive you on to great success and a great life.

Let me give you two examples of the magic of a vision. One is my example. The other comes from Abraham Lincoln. It was 1855 and he was responding to a young man by the name of Isham Reavis, who had written Lincoln asking if he could study law with him. Lincoln told him, in effect, about the magic of a vision.

My Dear Sir:

I have just reached home, and found your letter of the 23$^{rd}$. I am away from home too much of my time, for a young man to read law with me advantageously. If you are resolutely determined to make a lawyer of yourself, the thing is more than half done already. It is but a small matter whether you read with any body or not. I did not read with any one. Get the books, and read and study them till you understand them in their principal features; and that is the main thing. It is of no consequence to be in a large town while you are reading. I read at New Salem, which never had three hundred people living in it. The *books*, and your *capacity* for understanding them, are just the same in all places. Mr. Dummer is a very clever man and an excellent lawyer (much better than I, in law-learning); and I have no doubt he will cheerfully tell you what books to read, and also loan you the books.

Always bear in mind that your own resolution to succeed is more important than any other one thing.

Very truly your friend

A Lincoln

Abraham Lincoln gave this young man the formula to predict the future, at least his own future success: resolve. "Always bear in mind that your own resolution to succeed is more important than any other one thing," he wrote. Half the battle of any success is determining that you want to do it and that you will give your all to doing it. With that vision firmly in your mind, you are on the way to success.

This young man did, by the way, follow Lincoln's advice and went on to be a successful lawyer.

A vision is especially effective in predicting the future of a business venture. You'll recall that I started with a vision back in 1956—fanatical customer service delivered with integrity, at discounted prices. Let me give you a tangible example of the power, the magic of *that* vision. If the power of a vision can be measured by how long it has stayed relevant, how long that vision has remained a driving force, then my vision for Quill back in 1956 has turned out to be pretty potent.

Today if you go to the main campus of Quill Corporation outside Chicago, you see tangible evidence that my vision is still alive. Now, keep in mind that I haven't been there very often in more than seven years. But walk around Quill and you see banners and signs exhorting employees to be fanatical about customer service, to always do business the right way, with integrity, and to look for ways to cut costs. But signs are signs. Employees are people.

On a recent visit to Quill, I roamed through the various departments as I always used to do, talking with people, asking questions. Some were people who were at Quill when I was there. Others were new, hired after I had gone. Every one of them talked about how much they liked working at Quill. When asked, every one of them said the reason was because at Quill, business was done the right way, with integrity. They care about how employees are treated. This shapes how they treat each other. And it shapes how customers and suppliers are treated. Each and every one of these employees spoke about how business was always done the right way and how that made them feel good about coming to work.

They also talked about why Quill beats the pants off its competitors, why Quill is the most profitable center of Staples: fanatical customer service combined with a constant search for cost savings. Every one of the employees, from the old-timers who have been there three decades and more, to the new employees yet to celebrate their first-year anniversary, spoke of the company's commitment to customer service.

When we first started our web site, we instituted a rule at Quill: questions that came in online from customers are to be answered within four hours. Most companies strive for 24 hours—we insisted on four hours. That rule still exists today at Quill, and I'm told is still being met every day. Also Quill still strives to out-customer service every competitor. Quill employees order from competitors to see how long it takes for delivery. They also submit questions to competitors to see how long it takes to get an answer. Today, a half century after I founded Quill with a simple vision, one that I was sure would succeed, that vision is still being put into action every day by more than the 2,400 employees at Quill.

The magic of a vision—as a business owner I know that's the only way to predict the future. It's the vision inside you, the vision of where you want to take your business.

Now when talking about the magic of a vision, I am not talking about creating a business plan and then doing financial projections based on that plan. Ask any banker who is deciding whether to give a loan based on such business plans and financial projections, and he will probably tell you that the great majority of them are more works of fiction than they are predictors of the future.

To me, the magic of a vision is the growing realization of what can be. When I started Quill, I had no vision of creating the company we became. My only goal was to be able to make a living by peddling office products in the Chicago area. I didn't even envisage us becoming a mail order firm. I was just going door-to-door to every business I could find to try to sell them some products. The limit of my vision was that I really believed that I could make it happen by providing great customer service and discounted prices. So despite constant turndowns and a few successes, I just kept knocking on those doors.

It's not that I believe business plans and projections are unimportant, not at all. But they are only guidelines. They are, and should be, ever-evolving guidelines with some basic core beliefs that should stay steady.

Even becoming a mail order firm was just something that happened. It was not part of my vision. As I said earlier, we slid into being a mail order company. I believed in advertising and so I began sending out crude, one page advertising pieces. As time went on and as we could afford to pay for them, our advertising pieces became larger and professionally done. Then, one day we realized that we were getting so many phone calls from customers and prospects as a result of those pieces that we had to stay in most of the day to answer them and to take orders. But the basics stayed the same—discount pricing and great service. In the early days most of the competition were selling to small businesses at list prices.

As our business continued to grow, our vision of what we could become became even stronger. And as we envisioned what we wanted to be and where we wanted to get to, we began making plans for how to get there. We constantly talked about those plans with each other, with our accountant, our banker, and others. More and more, we defined who we were, what kind of company we were, and what we wanted our company to become.

And, most importantly, we began to measure every opportunity against that vision and to take advantage of or to reject those opportunities based on whether they would fit that vision. We focused like a laser beam on that ever-evolving vision.

Obviously, there were twists and turns in the road we chose to take, unforeseen problems and unforeseen opportunities, but by keeping that vision strongly in mind, we managed those twists and turns and kept growing, never catching up with that constantly evolving vision, but never too far behind it, either.

As we continued to grow and as more and more people came into the company, we made that vision a focal point of almost all of our conversations, talks, and written communications such as our company newsletter. We knew that if we were going to succeed, we had to share our vision with everyone in the company and get them to believe in it, too.

Earlier in this book I talked about the confidence to take risks, about how you don't go into business for yourself if you are too allergic to risk. Well, that doesn't change as your business grows. But, of course, once you start growing, you don't want to bet the ranch. The risks you take are the risks you know. If something fails, you can pay for it, walk away, and go on to the next idea. You get smarter about risks, but you take them. So another lesson: have confidence in your vision.

This became even more obvious to me as when, as I mentioned, I toured Quill years after I had left. Employees who joined

Quill long after we had sold the company still sounded like me and my brothers had 50 years before. All the crucial words that guided us when we were small, guided us as we grew into a big company, are still on the lips of people who work at Quill: words like customer service, integrity, watching costs. That final lesson is almost obvious: talk about your vision!

I know so many business owners who have a vision in their heads for their business, but whose employees are more likely to be able to recite the Torah than the vision of their boss. How can you possibly expect the people working for you to be pursuing the same vision—the vision that will make you profits—if you don't continually spread it?

It just became very obvious to me and my brothers that, if we wanted to become what we saw in our dreams, it was critical to share that vision. Without it and without everyone in the company believing in it, there would be no map that guided us and our people when decisions had to be made. Otherwise, every choice would look equally correct. Of course, you can't run a business that way. As someone once said, "Effort and courage are not enough without purpose and direction."

Or perhaps it was said best in *Alice in Wonderland*:

> "Would you tell me please, which way I have to go from here?" Alice asked.
> "That depends a good deal on where you want to get to," said the cat.
> "I don't much care where," said Alice.
> "Then it doesn't matter which way you go," said the cat.

I strongly believe that one of the biggest problems most companies (and most individuals) have is that they haven't thought through what they want out of life, and following that, what actions they must take, what sacrifices they must make, what opportunities they must grab in order to achieve their dream. As a result, they often choose ways that lead away from where they would really like to go.

The real magic of having a vision, a constantly evolving, constantly growing vision, is that it sharpens the focus of where you want to get to and it acts as a star in guiding you on your path there.

# Chapter 7

# Focus: Putting on the Blinders

There's a banner I once saw, hanging on the wall in my granddaughter's fifth grade classroom that read, "No one can be good at everything, but everyone can be good at something."

My grandchildren all excel in some areas. In others they don't do so well, indeed they struggle. And every time they struggle, their self-esteem takes a hit. So I certainly understand why the teacher put up that banner. He wanted his students to realize that they could be good at something and that actually no one was good at everything, including the top students in the class.

This banner could—actually should—go on the wall of every entrepreneur's, in fact every CEO's, office.

There are two lessons in this banner. The first is that every person has a talent that with hard work they could build into a very good business and life. The trick is just figuring out what that talent is and then working like hell to get the most out of that talent.

The second lesson, one that is especially relevant for all CEOs of companies from the smallest to the largest, is that just because you (or your company) are good in one particular area is no reason to believe you will be good at something else. This is a lesson that all too many CEOs, even the biggest, often don't learn until they make some very costly mistakes thinking that they are good at things outside their field of expertise.

I know a number of very successful businesspeople, some of whom started with nothing and built a net worth in the billions. But I don't know any geniuses. They are all, or at least the vast majority of them, pretty nice and pretty ordinary folks. One of them, one of the most successful people I know, has a learning disability. He can't, or won't, read legal documents, long reports, or even books. But he has succeeded beyond most of our wildest dreams. He built a huge company because of his drive and his focus on extraordinary customer service and the taking care of his people extraordinarily well as well as the finding of the most economic way possible of doing everything in his company so he could sell at very low prices with that great customer service.

Every single successful businessperson I know, most of whom started their businesses from scratch and with very little money, was very focused and very good at just a few things. That includes me. And it includes my second wife Goldie, who owned the largest woman-owned commercial real estate firm in the country before she sold it.

Neither of us made the number one deadly sin of many businesspeople. We didn't convince ourselves that we knew more than we actually did. We stuck with the message of that banner in that fifth grade classroom. And that, I believe, is the story of most successful entrepreneurs.

I once read a story I really liked, about an unusual focus. It's about a young girl with autism. The severity of autism ranges greatly but essentially it means that the individual has a developmental problem that impacts the normal development of the brain. A major result is difficulties in social interaction and communication skills.

Yet many autistic people are very smart and it is not unusual for an autistic child to find one thing and to focus almost exclusively on that one thing. The young girl in this story for some reason focused on cattle chutes. She read everything there was to read about cattle chutes. By the time she became an adult, she had read so much about them that she knew more about them than practically anyone else in the world. She became a very successful consultant on cattle chutes to companies all over the world.

As I said before and it bears repeating, in my opinion and from my experience, most successful businesspeople are not geniuses. They are no smarter than a lot of other people. (In fact, the saying "the A's and the B's work for the C's" may have some truth in it.)

But the successful ones just get into something and they work very hard at being the best they can possibly be in that area and at making their company the very best it can be. They outwork and outperform their competition in their particular field. And over the years they just keep learning how to be better and better at doing that. They never stop learning. They never commit the sin of thinking that they know everything there is to know about their field.

All resources—time, money, energy, expertise—are limited. Many businesspeople (and the government) forget this and spread these resources thinly. They fail to focus their limited resources in their core competencies, their core business, and therefore fail to achieve the success they could have.

The amount of time we are allotted on this earth is finite. Deduct the amount of time from birth to beginning your career. Then deduct the amount of time from retirement to death. What's left is about one-half your lifetime. Then if you deduct the time you sleep, spend with your family, go on vacations, and so on you begin to realize how little time you really have to achieve success. But if you really zero in and focus your time, energy, and resources, that is more than enough time to achieve your dream.

So as much as possible in your career do only those things that will help you achieve that dream. Every time an opportunity comes up when you might have to invest your finite resources of time, money, and energy, just ask yourself if that opportunity is really central to your vision, your dream. If not, then you should ignore it, no matter how tantalizing it may be.

And that is why I believe a mission statement is so crucial to success. A well-thought-out mission statement should be the touchstone for keeping you and everyone in your company focused. It gives you a reference point, and every time you have an opportunity of investing your time, money, or energy into something, look at that mission statement. If it is a very good fit, go for it. If it's a loose fit, be very careful. And if it doesn't fit at all, stay away.

In business, you should be pouring all your energies and other resources into a very targeted effort. The worst advice for a businessperson is to not "put all your eggs in one basket." A much better piece of advice came from Andrew Carnegie, an industrialist and philanthropist, who went from being a poor immigrant to one of the world's richest men. His advice was to "Concentrate; put all your eggs in one basket and watch that basket."

But if you do focus and build a successful business, you may fall into another trap. I call it "the arrogance of success." Some successful people really do begin to feel that their success proves their brilliance and this expresses itself in many ways.

It often plays itself out when mergers and acquisitions take place. Almost every day we read about acquisitions taking place, and then later we read about companies shedding their acquisitions to get back to their "core competencies." The merger of AOL and Time Warner was just one such example. Among a lot of ballyhoo about how they were going to redefine media, they merged. Today, they are separated and back to working at their core competencies.

We experienced this ourselves. There were three dominant office products mail order firms in the country: ourselves, Viking, and Reliable.

Reliable sold to a very successful contract stationer with no experience in mail order. That contract stationer took over completely and soon Reliable basically disappeared as a competitor. Mail order was not a core competency for them.

Viking sold to the largest, at the time, office products superstore, Office Depot. Office Depot moved Viking's headquarters from California to Florida, in the process losing many of the people who had helped make Viking successful. They also combined warehouses and substituted a lot of the products they sold in their stores for the similar (but not equal) products that Viking sold through their catalogs. Viking, which had built their business on fanatical customer service, was soon providing the much less fanatical service of Office Depot and products that weren't up to the Viking standards.

As a result, Viking began to slip as a competitor and in January 2006, it disappeared as a separate entity. It was just a part of Office Depot and had lost everything that made it unique. Again, mail order was not a core competency for them.

On the other hand, when we were negotiating with Tom Stemberg and Ron Sargent from Staples about the sale of Quill, we set some preconditions. First, we required that Quill be kept as an independently operating separate entity with the Quill people we put in charge operating it. We also negotiated that our people would get equal or better benefits.

As a result, today Quill has grown substantially under the leadership of our people who had been there for many years. (If we had realized how good they were, we could have learned to play golf before we retired.)

I stayed on for a year and a half after the sale to help in the transition. And while Tom and Ron were good to their word, I did have to spend time fighting off newly minted MBAs from Staples who wanted to come in and dictate how this very successful company, Quill, should be run.

Today Quill is the most successful division of Staples, contributing to Staples' profit at a rate way out of proportion to Quill's percentage of Staples' sales.

See, Staples didn't make the mistake of being seduced by the arrogance of success. They kept Quill a separate entity and even copied some of Quill's expertise. Many other successful companies often acquire businesses outside their field of expertise, or even within that field of expertise but with a completely different culture and approach and then start to change these successful companies to fit their model and culture and usually they end up ruining the company they acquired.

I've often wondered why someone would acquire a very successful company, buying it because of its success, and then promptly begin to change the very things that made it such a success. Why? In my opinion, it's pure arrogance, to a monumental degree.

There are thousands of such examples. One is Fleet Boston Financial, New England's dominant bank group, which in 2003 began shedding $10 billion worth of acquisitions that they deemed "businesses not critical to our core mission." In other words, these were businesses they didn't really know how to run, businesses that were not within their core competencies. Just imagine the amount of executive time and money that went into the acquisition of these businesses and then the disposition of them. It has to be staggering. Money and time that could have been so much better spent building their own business.

Another good example is Amazon, the 800-pound Internet gorilla. In an article titled "Amazon's Core Problem" (*Wall Street Journal*, April 2, 2001), Chris Zook summed up the problem of businesses that stop doing what they do so well and start doing what they *think* they can do well. It's worth quoting Zook, a director at a global management consulting firm: "We estimate that the odds of success for a major business growth initiative far from a strong core are low, probably less than 10 percent." Note those odds: 9 out of 10 chance of failing if you *don't* stick with what you do best, if you *don't* focus, if you *do* make the mistake of thinking you are smarter than you are.

Zook writes, "Amazon's troubles with its core are hardly unique." He goes on to outline three common pitfalls when companies expand beyond their core. While you are not the size of Fleet Boston Financial or Amazon (who is?), his points apply to even the smallest businesses.

1. "Failure to *define* the core business. If you misdefine your core business, your odds of profitable growth drop like a stone." He goes on to talk about the risks of defining too broadly or too narrowly, although I would always prefer to err on the side of a bit more narrowly: "Over 87 percent of the most successful growth companies we studied had a single, dominant core business that they expanded systematically and organically. Less than three percent of sustained growth companies had at least three strong cores."

2. "Failure to strengthen the core to its fullest potential before expanding aggressively." Here Zook says, "Getting the full profit potential from your core must take priority." Basically, what he is saying here is that if you have only 3 percent or 5 percent or even 10 percent of the market you are in, you have a lot better chance of sustained growth if you focus very strongly on your own market. Of course, if you have 75 percent or more of your market, or if you are in a declining market then you probably do want to look at other markets. I doubt that this applies to you. It never did to us at Quill, although over the years we did keep expanding lines by adding other kinds of products our core customers used. For example, although office products was always our core, we expanded into janitorial supplies, food for the break room, ad specialties, and more. But the way we ran our business, being mail order only to only businesses, with great prices, and fantastic customer service always remained the same.

3. "Failure to anticipate the challenges of movements away from the core."

   I can tell you from my own experience about how challenging it is to move beyond your core. After we sold Quill, I invested in and then finally bought another firm, Successories. Its core business is business to business (B to B) mail order, just as Quill's was. I thought it would be easy to turn this failing company around. But it was not only B to B mail order, it also had 50 or 60 retail stores around the country (with no one on staff who knew retail marketing), 15 or so franchisees (again, with no one on staff who knew the franchisee business), the remainders of a failed golf business, and more. The basic product line—motivational posters and other motivational products—was great. Its basic problem, very different from what went on at Quill, was that the repeat business factor was very low. On top of all that, they were a very small public company while I was accustomed to running a privately held company. Believe me, I did not anticipate the challenges of this new business venture, which I eventually purchased and took private. We got rid of everything we were doing except the business to business mail order segment plus a few franchisees. After four or five years, we are beginning to turn the company around, adding products such as ad specialties, which have a higher repeat factor. And we are profitable.

Zook concludes the article by quoting American Express CEO Ken Chenault: "Through our long history, we have seldom made any money when we have departed from the core."

Right here, I would like to mention my "rope theory." I believe very strongly that you should stick with your core business, but also I believe that you can expand on your core if you do it carefully. Expanding into areas not related to your core is like adding different strings that are not interwoven and that can individually be easily broken. But if each string you add is one that is close to your core string and can be interwoven with it, you can build a rope that eventually becomes so strong that it can't be broken. Each string is closely related to the others and adds strength to the whole.

Now, here's an example of someone who got it right. Gordon Segal is founder and CEO of Crate and Barrel. Years ago Gordon and his wife Carole traveled to Europe and fell in love with Scandinavian household products. When they returned, they decided to go into the retail business selling them. They opened their first small store in a bohemian neighborhood near downtown Chicago. They had no money for fancy shelving and fixtures, so they decided to just display the merchandise on the crates and barrels that they arrived from Europe in. And that's how the Segals got the name of their store, Crate and Barrel.

Fanatically focusing on this core competency, Gordon and Carole built their business. Today, they have 145 stores nationwide. They employ more than 7,000 people and have sales of about $750 million per year and growing. Crate and Barrel is a profitable and well-run company. The only thing they ever added to their core concept was to establish a mail-order arm of their business.

Their story is very much like those of all of the successful businesspeople I know. They started out very modestly, learning and growing as they went along. And Gordon is, just like every other successful entrepreneur I know, very driven, very hands-on, very consumed by the business, and very, very focused.

My second example of somebody who did it the right way comes from the world of sports. Bart Conner won the Olympic gold medal in gymnastics in 1984. Bart was a classmate of my daughter Judy, who was also a gymnast. Judy was good, but not in Bart's class. His whole life was focused on gymnastics. He worked out for hours on end. He and his parents spent many an evening watching films of the top Olympian gymnasts of the day, playing the films over and over again. When it came time to choose a college, they chose the school that had the very best gymnastic program in the country. They couldn't understand why Judy didn't make her college choice using the same criteria.

On the other hand, I've seen up close what happens when you don't focus. As I've mentioned elsewhere, but it bears repeating, a friend of mine took over his father-in-law's business. It had been started in the very early 1900s by his father-in-law's father. At the time, just when I was setting up shop, it was a good and profitable business.

Well, when my friend Vic took over the business, it didn't get his unyielding focus. See, Vic loved to play the stock market. He kept a television set on his desk that was always tuned to a channel reporting stock prices all day long. You can guess the moral of this story. While he was watching the television and not watching his business—the business his father-in-law's father started nearly a century ago—went bankrupt.

Vic's story also proves that old truism I mentioned before: "You can always make more by investing in your own business than you can by investing anywhere else." I realize it doesn't always work out that way, but I would sure bet on it, as long as you stay focused like a laser beam on your business.

I took this truism to heart. Outside of one small, brief investment in a mutual fund early on, I never invested in the stock market, never had the slightest interest in it. Every nickel we made went back into the business to help grow it. It wasn't until a few years before we sold Quill, when we had accumulated a great deal of money in the business, that we began to invest in bonds and money market funds. Buying another business didn't interest us, because Quill was still growing. So we began to take some profits out of the business. Of course my friend Vic and some others thought we were dumb. But after we sold the business, financial advisors told us it was a pretty smart investment strategy since the business itself provided plenty of exposure to the equity market and investing in bonds was a good way to diversify.

How would I sum up this lesson? I'd say, choose your niche, focus on it, and become a real expert at your chosen focus. The best entrepreneurs never lose focus. They shape their business, their every action around it. Their policies, promotional activities, the people they hire, the books and magazines they read, the seminars and meetings they attend, even the types of customer they seek, all and everything are focused in this one area. The result is that soon they not only have a product or service to sell, they have something special, something more. They have expertise that adds tremendous value to what they are selling and how they run their businesses. It's that expertise and knowledge that puts them head and shoulders above their competition.

Successful entrepreneurs differ in many ways. They do, I believe, share a common characteristic, a real belief that they, themselves, are responsible for their own actions and that through their own actions and by focusing their efforts, they can make the good things they want to happen come to pass.

One of my favorite sayings is "Actions have consequences, and each of us is responsible for our own actions." This is very true in building a great business and building a great life.

It takes a lot of things—some talent, a lot of ambition and hard work, plus some luck. It also takes a lot of focus.

# Chapter 8

# Concentrate on Your Customer

"He who confers the greatest service at the least expense, we will crown with honor and clothe with riches." This is a great thought to keep in mind every single day and something that should be a part of all your planning. In a free economic system, such as ours, the customer is the one who decides what he or she wants and is willing to pay for.

Our economic system, capitalism, is the envy of the world, as it is the only system that works. Simply put, it's based on the free exchange of goods or services among willing people. "Free" and "willing" are the key words. It is the most American of concepts, and what it means for you, the entrepreneur, is simple: you must produce a product or provide a service that people need or want and are willing to pay for. But since a lot of companies are probably producing or providing the same or similar items and services, it means you must do something more, give the customer more, to get them to buy from you instead of someone else. Lower prices are one way. But very often others can match those lower prices. In my experience, battling on cost alone, while important, is not enough to win the war with competition. What is, though, is great, actually fantastic fanatical customer service. And for some reason if you give that kind of customer service, you won't have many competitors matching you.

Many companies and organizations talk about customer service. A good many even give decent customer service, most of the time, anyway. And too many provide terrible customer service. But only a very few provide outstanding, world class customer service all of the time, the type of customer service customers talk about, rave about. How do those very few do it?

It's not complicated nor is it hard to understand. But it does take a lot of hard, persistent effort, day in, day out effort.

By the way when I talk about customers, I mean both external customers as well as internal customers. The internal customers are just as important as the external ones because when they are happy and well serviced, they have an impact on external customers, either directly or through others in the organization.

To start with, the top people in the company *must* have an absolute conviction that great customer service never costs. It always makes money for the company. As a matter of fact, at Quill we found that the better the service we gave, the less it cost. For example, if a customer has a complaint or problem, and it is taken care of *immediately*, you eliminate additional calls from the customer trying to find out what is happening and therefore additional expense, not to mention the fact that you have a happier customer who is likely to buy a lot more from you.

One time at Quill, as I was walking through the customer service department, I saw a large pile of paper in a basket and asked what it was about. They told me that these were customer service problems that they hadn't been able to get to yet because the phones were so busy. I sort of blew my stack and went to the manager of the department and insisted that he put as many people on it as he had to, using whatever overtime necessary to get caught up.

They did, and within a week they were totally current. After that the same number of people who were originally in customer service were able to stay current because the number of calls decreased significantly. Why? Because people weren't calling back two or three times to find out what was happening with their problem. See, it's a simple equation: do it very well the first time, or fix the problem quickly when it shows up, and you save money because you save time. And you have far happier customers.

In many companies they talk about giving good (why don't they use the word *great?*) customer service, but when it comes to investing the money to make it happen, they back off and don't "walk the talk." And that sends a message throughout the organization.

Fantastic customer service also pays off big time in customer retention and repeat business and in word-of-mouth advertising as your amazed and very pleased customers tell others about your company and how much easier it is to deal with your company when something does go wrong. Nothing else in your marketing plan will give you a bigger payback in the long run. I know a young man—well, young to me—who runs a service-oriented company. Not long ago a long-time customer complained about the hourly rate he was charged for a project. He didn't feel that the employee who explained the project to him had accurately explained the costs to him. The entrepreneur immediately slashed the bill in half. The result of cutting an approximately $10,000 bill to $5,000? A $100,000 project came in shortly after from this same client. Not that you should just cut your bills if a customer complains, but if there is some justification for their complaint, act quickly to satisfy them.

Great customer service also reduces operating costs. Let me give you an example. For some reason, at Quill our whole system of returns and credits wasn't at the top of someone's agenda as a customer service issue. So it took several days to check in the returns and then even longer before the credit memo was issued. As a result, we sometimes were getting calls from angry customers who were being dunned for money on merchandise they had already returned. And that took more work to trace down the problem, straighten it out, and notify the customer.

The solution was simple. We insisted that all returns be processed the day they were received and the credit memo issued the following day. It took extra manpower to catch up, but once again, once we had caught up, it took just the original manpower we were using before to stay caught up.

The concept I arrived at as a result of all this was "If you are going to do a day's work in a day, then you might as well do today's work today."

The lesson is that if you respond quickly to customer requests and complaints, it will guarantee savings in operating costs and almost surely result in additional repeat business and great word-of-mouth advertising. You can easily audit your level of customer service by walking around and talking to people who handle customer complaints, by reading incoming mail or e-mails, and by listening in on some of the customer service calls.

To provide fantastic customer service, you need to understand what really great customer service means to the customer. Sure, it includes delivering the merchandise or the service you provide quickly, but that isn't enough. It must be done well. The order must be shipped complete and accurately. But that is only one aspect of a much, much larger picture. Answering the phones within three rings (preferably one ring) in a very pleasant manner is another aspect. Resolving problems quickly, while the customer is on the line, or if that absolutely isn't possible, within hours, is another aspect. Everything, from the offer on through to seeing that the customer is totally satisfied with the purchase and with all of their dealings with everyone in the organization should be a great experience for the customer.

I know one small businessman who routinely calls his customers and asks, "How are we doing?" He makes sure dealing with his company is a great experience and, whenever he learns it is not, fixes whatever the problem is right away.

Another, often overlooked, aspect of really great customer service goes back to the old country store where the proprietor knew every customer by name and knew what they had bought in the past, what their preferences were. That aspect of customer service was lost as companies grew larger and customers seemed more remote. But with the advent of computers it has become possible once again to really know your customers on a very individual basis and know their needs and preferences.

When computers first came on the market, one of the major predictions was that they would depersonalize business. But as with most other predictions, that was 180 degrees out of whack. Computers, properly used, have made it possible to deal even more personally with customers on a one-to-one basis. If you work at it, you can develop programs so you know all about the customer, the name of the person doing the purchasing, and what they have bought in the past, all of which allow you to service them better and even allow you to make suggestions of what else they might want and much, much more. You see it in action when you buy books or rent movies online. "If you liked such and such book (or movie), then you might also like X, Y, or Z." Go to Amazon.com and you'll see it.

Having a passion for customer service means always designing and redesigning systems and procedures with the customer in mind. That means the phone system, the many computer systems, invoicing and shipping procedures—every system and procedure in the company must be designed with one major question always being, "How will this affect customer service?" You must work hard to develop systems and ways of doing things that provide customers with a perfect experience so you not only meet but actually exceed their expectations. And that's the key word, "exceed." Rarely are people impressed when you meet their expectations but always are they impressed, and enthusiastic about referring their friends, when you exceed those expectations.

3M understood all of this when they changed how they handled the return of damaged or outdated goods. They cut costs and improved customer service at the same time. With the old way, when a dealer wanted to return damaged merchandise, the local sales rep had to go in and examine it. Then, with his approval, a request for permission to make the return was sent to headquarters in Minneapolis. This approval then went through several hands for further approval. If approved, a return authorization was sent to the customer, who then returned the merchandise and waited for his credit memo or check. What a lot of work for even a small return.

3M's solution, once they focused on it, was to have the salesperson go in and examine the goods. If the salesperson felt the return was justified, he or she wrote a check out on the spot and told the dealer to destroy the merchandise or donate it to a local charity.

Wow! What a difference in customer satisfaction *and* what fantastic savings in cost—to both the dealer and to 3M.

At Quill, we had a similar program in action when the cost to return the merchandise (freight and labor) exceeded the value of the merchandise. We would simply tell the customer, on the phone, to donate the merchandise to their local charity and we would send them a credit or a replacement. Not only did it save money, but it made the customer feel great. You can't believe how many times I heard about that policy from friends of mine who had experienced it or who had other friends who had experienced it. Talk about word-of-mouth advertising! I don't recall ever hearing of a case where this policy was abused.

And just think about renting a car these days. If you are a preferred customer, the auto rental bus drops you off at your vehicle, where it is ready to go. No lines to stand in. No paperwork to do. Then when you drop off the car, an agent looks at your gas meter and prints out your credit card charge on the spot. No going into the office. No standing in line.

Computers make checking out of a hotel equally easy. Checking in at the airport at the new automated check-in kiosks is simple. You can apply the same tactics in your company if you think about it and work at it.

In all these examples, costs were cut *and* customer service was improved. At Quill we were always trying to find ways to cut costs by improving the efficiency of our operations. But whenever we set about developing a new system to do that, we always asked ourselves how it would affect customer service. If it would hurt customer service, we wouldn't do it, regardless of the fact that it would save us some money in operations. But the fact of the matter was that once we really dug into the problem, we found that we could design the system not only to be more efficient but also to actually improve customer service. You just have to keep both goals in mind and insist on both of them being met. Too often we look at things only from the viewpoint of *our* systems, *our* needs, *our* problems without including the viewpoint of the customer, which should always be the overriding factor.

Once your organization becomes truly focused on providing fantastic customer service, it begins to happen almost automatically. But it must permeate every level of the company and people must feel they have the authority to really make it happen.

Let me give you an example of how this worked at Quill. A customer had ordered some merchandise that he needed for a presentation. The day before the presentation was to take place, the customer called frantically complaining that they hadn't yet received the merchandise. The customer service rep who took the call was smart enough and confident enough in his authority to serve the customer to say, "I'll go to the warehouse now and get the order replaced, and we'll run it over to the airport and get it on the first plane to your city. It will be there tonight."

The order was for about $300 and the cost to replace it and get it there in time was somewhat more than that. Was it a waste of money? When my brothers and I found out about what the rep had done, we didn't think so. We felt it was an investment that would pay off big in terms of keeping that customer. And we were sure that customer would talk about it to others for years. We even, personally, complimented that customer service rep in front of many others for doing a great job.

This rep felt empowered to make this decision because he was reading right out of our mission statement. The pursuit of great customer service should be part of your mission statement. It should be a major strategy along with other strategies for building the business. Whenever possible, it should be part of bonus goals. People should be publicly recognized and congratulated when they do something extra-ordinary in the way of customer service. And as for those people who can't, or won't, give great customer service, well, they are simply working for the wrong company.

So for your product or service, how do you determine what really great customer service is? The simplest and most obvious way is to begin an ongoing program of asking your customers what they expect in the way of customer service. Examine all the customer complaints and customer returns (and the notes that often come with them) to unearth problems that are correctible, thus often finding out what the customer wants and improving your customer service. Be constantly on the lookout for what other companies are doing. When you are shopping or going to a restaurant or are serviced in any manner, think about the service you are getting, good or bad. And, whenever you see something that you think is fantastic, copy it! You may have to adapt it a bit to fit your organization, but don't be shy about copying. Good ideas come from everywhere.

Also think of new things customers never even knew they wanted. In today's fast changing world, new technologies constantly make possible new ways to service customers—new ways to provide them with what they want. Be on the lookout for them and introduce them as quickly as possible. You will amaze and please your customers and keep them coming back to you.

That's really the bottom line of customer service: as they say, it always costs a lot more to get a new customer than it does to keep one. And that is exactly what fantastic customer service will do: keep your customers loyal to you and, by word of worth, bring in more.

# Chapter 9

# There is a Better Way

When Fred Smith, the founder of FedEx was in college, he wrote a paper about how society was being computerized and how that was going to change the way things had to be distributed and moved. He says he didn't get a very good grade on the paper and he let it lie. After college he went into the Marine Corps and observed how wastefully product was being handled and how "almost invariably all of the supplies were in the wrong place for where they were needed." That experience crystallized the idea that had been in his paper. He came up with an integrated air and ground system for delivering packages, and FedEx was born.

United Parcel Service had been in business for 66 years (1907) before a young college graduate, ex-Marine came up with this "better way" (1973) to deliver small packages. United Parcel was a giant at the time and owned the small package delivery business nationwide. Today they are battling a tough, big competitor, FedEx, who wouldn't be in business if United Parcel hadn't been so enamored with their own system and had looked for that better way themselves.

Here's a golden truth for every entrepreneur to remember: as smart as you may be, and whether you are just starting or you have been in the business for a long time, there is always a better way to do almost everything. Those who forget that truth may be heading for extinction. Just look around. Montgomery Ward, once a giant in mail order and retail is out of business. Sears is a much reduced entity. General Motors, Ford, and Chrysler are no longer the dominant auto manufacturers in the world, or even in the United States. Xerox thought they had the copier market all tied up with their big machines and their charges of so much a copy. Then the Japanese came along with inexpensive small copiers and Xerox lost a big part of their market. There are hundreds, thousands of similar examples. All have one thing in common. They weren't constantly looking for *the* better way, and someone else came up with it. It doesn't happen to just big companies. It happens to small ones, also.

I can pinpoint the moment a company begins its decline. That's the moment the leaders in a company begin to think that they are doing things very well and that there is little room for improvement or change. Unfortunately, this is an all too frequent occurrence in too many companies, and in too many industries. I could even argue, frankly, that it's true for many countries.

We haven't even begun to tap the potential of the computer to help us do things better. Let's take an obvious example, the 9-11 destruction of the Twin Towers in New York. There was plenty of information available about the threat, about people who might carry out the threat, even about some of these people taking flying lessons, learning how to fly but never interested in learning how to land. All the information was there. But it was never put together in a way that pinpointed the who, the what, and the how. But it could have been. There was a better way of using computers and sharing information to pull all that information together.

Old businesses die because they become ossified and don't (can't?) change. New businesses start and flourish, often with a new concept. That was certainly the case at Quill. Office products had been sold practically forever. When we entered the business, they were being sold through smallish mom-and-pop office supply stores and through contract stationers with salesmen on the street. We introduced mail order (certainly not a new idea) into the industry and became very successful.

Later, Tom Stemberg introduced mass merchandising at very low prices into the industry and built Staples into the multibillion dollar business it is today. Why didn't someone within the industry introduce either one of those concepts? The answer is relatively easy. It's because they were making a living at what they were doing and they were busy dealing with the daily problems. But even more importantly, every day when they woke up, they didn't ask themselves, "Is there a better way?"

Most of you reading this book are probably too young to remember the days when one would drive into a gas station and an attendant would come out, fill your tank, wash your windshield, and check your oil. (Unless they lived in New Jersey where, for reasons that make no economic sense, self-service gas stations are against the law.) Then someone realized that most people just wanted gas at the lowest price possible and came up with the idea of self-service, using your credit card at the gas pump. There was a better way. The same was true of grocery stores. My father-in-law and his brother owned a small grocery store. Customers would come in and ask for products on their shopping list. My father-in-law and his brother would take them off the shelves themselves, bag them, and ring up the sale. Compare that with the much lower-priced self-service food stores of today. Some smaller grocers changed, grew, and survived. My father-in-law and his brother didn't and went out of business.

Whole industries keep changing practically overnight. A new idea, a new method of selling, a new technology hits an industry and suddenly companies that have been in business for decades are gone. New ones pop up. Some jobs disappear and new ones appear. All of these changes are happening faster and faster because each new advance, or discovery, fosters hundreds of other new advances. Think about what the Internet has meant to business. We are living in exciting times and a business owner's mind-set must change if he is to remain competitive.

Marshall Field, the legendary retailer, built a great retailing empire in Chicago, partially on the concept of "Give the lady what she wants." This dealt mostly with the concept of customer service. But today that wouldn't be sufficient. Today in almost every business, part of the concept must be "Give the lady what she doesn't even yet know she wants."

How many of us knew even just 10 years ago that we wanted global positioning systems in our cars? Yet today they are almost becoming a standard item. In a few years they will be. Fifteen years ago, how many of us knew that we wanted a cell phone, one we could carry in our pocket or purse and get calls practically wherever we were?

When I first started in business, I was a salesman in the food industry, calling on distributors across the country. Something new was just starting: frozen foods. Restaurants weren't demanding them. Restaurant owners didn't foresee the advent of frozen foods. But suddenly there they were, and restaurants were putting in freezers (something new) and were discontinuing buying ice. The smart ice distributors realized they had warehouses with thick, insulated walls, had salesmen calling on restaurants, and had an office staff. They made the change to becoming frozen food distributors. The not-so-smart ice distributors—well, when was the last time you ordered ice delivered to your home?

Or take portion control, another concept that started about that time. Restaurants were serving jelly in jars or on plates. Someone came up with the idea of packaging jelly in individual small serving containers. That was a better way. Those who introduced it profited mightily from it, and those manufacturers of jelly who didn't provide portion control products lost a large market share.

The list could go on and on. From such mundane products as toilet seat covers in public washrooms to the most sophisticated computer-driven items, there is always a better way. For example, one revolution that is just taking place is the use of computer chips in almost every product. The bar code, which was a revolutionary new technology not too long ago, is already being replaced by computer chips that will do so much more.

Yes, there is *always* a better way. Start-up entrepreneurs, with very little to try to protect in terms of infrastructure and "sunk" investments, are in a great position to come up with something a little different that will allow them to compete and grow a business. More established entrepreneurs within an industry have the same opportunity if they would just keep reminding themselves that they are not as smart as they think.

Large companies with a big infrastructure and a rigid organization are probably the least likely to initiate such changes. They and their people have too much to protect. Unions, of course, are notoriously against any change. They have jobs to protect.

As a final note, I believe we Americans should stop worrying about outsourcing of jobs and about lower-cost foreign manufacturers stealing jobs. With the same amount of energy and focus, we should be zeroing in on all the better ways there are to get things done. In one of the most glaring examples, our steel industry always bellyaches about competition from lower-cost overseas competitors and demands protection from our government through high-import duties. But they have done very little to find a better way of producing steel here in this country and a better way of running their companies so that they could compete.

From cost savings in the way things are done within the company, to ways of serving customers better, to better methods of distribution, to better systems of production, to almost everything we do in our businesses, there are better ways to do what we are doing. Those entrepreneurs who constantly seek the better ways and are willing to trash the old ways will win.

# Chapter 10

# Plotting Your Course
# with Strategic Planning

Once you have developed your vision and your mission statement, and you know exactly what you want to be (and what you don't want to be), the next step is to determine how you will get there. That is called strategic planning. You have to develop a road map that will take you where you want to go. And once that is done, you will need to develop the plan for implementing the strategies. Businesses that are truly successful are driven by a powerful vision of what they want to be and a solid plan of how they want to get there. Plus they have a strong entrepreneur constantly pushing and pulling to help power that vision and plan.

When I first started Quill, the strategic planning was very simple. As I have already said, my mission was to make a living and my strategies were quite simple. I would go out every day and knock on as many (business) doors as I could. I would offer 10 percent, 15 percent, or 20 percent off the list prices shown in the wholesaler's catalog. When I received orders, I would order the merchandise from the wholesaler the next morning, pick it up that afternoon, and ship it that afternoon for next-day delivery. The invoices would be typed up (at home) that night and sent out the next day. It would be tiring, sometimes exhausting, but it was always exhilarating. I believed in that initial vision and I believed I could make it happen.

It was a simple strategy and it worked. Of course, as we grew and our mission statement became more precise and our ambitions larger, our strategic planning became more important and more clearly defined. But the basics of aggressively looking for more business and of providing great customer service remained the same.

Over the years, as we did more and more strategic planning, I discovered some basic rules that must be followed in order for your strategic planning to be successful.

The first rule, and the cardinal one, is to "keep it simple." Keeping your strategic planning simple will pay off. Your plans may not be easy to achieve, requiring a lot of attention and effort, but they can be simple in concept.

A second cardinal rule is avoiding what I call "the candy store syndrome."

Just picture a kid in a candy store with his limited amount of money clutched in his sweaty hand, anxiously glancing back and forth, first at this candy bar and then at that one, and then at the chewing gum, and so on. He's almost immobilized because so many things look so good.

That's not too different from so many people in business with limited resources and seemingly unlimited opportunities. You can drive yourself nuts trying to make up your mind about what opportunities to pursue. Some businesspeople spend their whole business lives in this condition. First, they pursue one opportunity and then another and another and so on. They keep frittering away their resources of time, money, and energy and not making much progress. It's a great waste of energy—and of opportunity.

The most successful (and the happiest) businesspeople I know are those who decide early exactly what kind of business they want to have and how they want to run it. They pick their niche and then focus all their energies at becoming the best they can be in that particular niche. They may not pick exactly the right niche the first time, but they are probably close enough that with continued modifications, they reach the right choice. Those modifications come only as a result of trial, error, feedback, and more trial.

So your strategic planning should be highly focused on exactly what you want to be and you should consider only strategies that will get you there. Recall the rope theory I mentioned earlier.

A third cardinal rule of strategic planning is to "focus on the significant few, not the insignificant many." This rule is probably one of the most ignored rules in business as well as in our personal lives. We always seem to be so busy that we don't seem to have the time to do some things we really want to. But the truth of the matter is that if we focused on those few things that were really important and ignored those many that were, really, unimportant, we could achieve so much more. And we wouldn't be so stressed out, either.

In business there are usually a few very significant actions that could really "move the needle," make a major change. In your strategic planning, it is critical to decide what those "significant few" really are and make sure that you plan to focus resources and effort on them. As for the insignificant many, decide which need doing and assign some resources to them. But even more important, decide on those that really don't need doing and that won't make any difference, or very little difference, if they are not done, and don't waste resources on them.

With those cardinal rules in mind, let's move on to another step in your strategic planning. That is consider your marketplace, your competition, and their strengths and weaknesses. Consider your own strengths and weaknesses. Your goal should be to decide what the market, or a good enough segment of the market, really wants and how you might be able to provide that better than your competitors can. It could be breadth of line, quality, faster delivery, innovative products, or any number of other things.

One of the most unique strategic approaches I have seen was from a very successful medical supply house. Their competition, Abbott Laboratories, Baxter Labs, and others were formidable competitors with a lot more money so they could have distribution centers all around the country and could provide fast delivery of products, which is so critical to hospitals. So this company came up with the strategy of putting their products into hospital supply rooms on a consignment basis. The hospitals would then pay for the products as they used them and the company would replenish the supplies as needed. Instead of having to build and staff expensive distribution centers, this company used the hospitals' supply rooms (rent free) and the hospital personnel as their distribution centers. A brilliant and, more importantly, very profitable strategy.

For the hospitals, this strategy improved their cash flow, not having to buy and pay in advance of their need for the product. And they were always "in stock." It's a strategy that has catapulted this company to great success. But when you think about it, it wasn't such an original strategy. In fact, for example, you experience it every time you stay at a hotel. They have a minibar stocked with liquor, candy, and snacks. You take what you want, the hotel replaces it the next day, and you pay for it when you check out. Indeed, the strategy goes back further than that, to the traditional consignment shops where people bring their wares to sell. The store pays nothing until the article is sold. This very successful medical supply company simply had the idea of taking the old consignment shop strategy to hospitals.

If you really understand your market, your competitors, and your own strengths and weaknesses, you can come up with a pretty good strategy for success. Basically, there are two approaches that you can use. One is to do more of what you have been doing; if it has been successful, it can lead you to even greater success. The other approach is to set some seemingly impossible goals and then make some radical changes to try to achieve those goals. At Quill we sort of followed a combination of the two systems. What we had been doing was working quite well and we kept perfecting it. But at the same time, we set some very high stretch goals in some specific areas.

For example, as I have already mentioned, our promise to customers was that we would *ship* all orders within eight to 32 hours. But as competition heated up, we decided that this wasn't good enough. So we decided we needed to improve on our strategy of fast shipment. Our target, which we achieved, was the seemingly impossible goal to *ship* all orders received by 4 P.M. (later raised to

6 P.M.) that same day. After we set that goal, we found ways to achieve it.

But we took this idea even further. We decided that this still wasn't good enough. What was important was how quickly the customer *received* the goods. So we made a strategic decision that we wanted to provide *next-day delivery*. With one warehouse located in Lincolnshire, Illinois, that was a practical impossibility. It took UPS four days to deliver to California. Using air express was impractical because our products generally were heavy and low-cost. So we opened a West Coast distribution center and eventually ended up with nine distribution centers around the country, providing next day delivery almost everywhere in the country.

The lesson here is that if you have a very clear mission and then develop an ever-evolving strategy to achieve it, it can lead to great success. There will be twists and turns in the road as the market changes, as new competition emerges, as some things don't work, but basically if you follow the cardinal rules of keeping it simple, avoiding the candy store syndrome, and focusing on the significant few and not the insignificant many, you maximize your chance of achieving your goals.

But that assumes good implementation of your strategy. So let's talk about that in Chapter 11.

# Chapter 11

# Implementation: Making It Happen

Carl von Clausewitz once said, "A simple plan well executed is better than a brilliant plan poorly executed." In my many years of business, I've learned some of the keys to making sure a good plan is well executed.

It's like the dieter's fallacy. How many people have you known who announce a diet but don't do the real work of sensible eating and regular exercise over a sustained period of time? Great plan, bad implementation is the failure of most dieters. And then there are those who want to improve their golf game but don't take lessons and don't spend the hours necessary on the driving range.

Well, that is the same thing that happens in our business lives. You can make all the plans you want, brilliant or simple, and unless they are executed well—and consistently—they won't make a bit of difference in your business. What I have learned in my years in business is that there are some very basic concepts and disciplines that are necessary for successful implementation of any strategic plan.

The first is that *everyone* in the company from the custodian to the CEO must know what the strategy is and what part they can play in it. They must believe in it and become enthusiastic about it. Making that happen requires constant communication. The plan has to be written out and explained to everyone, not just once but over and over. It practically has to become a mantra within the company, something that is repeated to aid concentration, in this case, concentration on achieving the goals set out.

How the strategic plan is implemented—that is, the actual tactics—must be owned by the employees. In larger companies, each department must be allowed to work out the tactics. In smaller companies, groups of employees do so. But what can't happen is that the tactics are simply dictated by the boss.

These tactics, when broken down by department and/or by individual, amount to a bunch of small steps that add up to grand achievements. Nothing about it is brain surgery. Once broken down into these small, tactical steps, it becomes much simpler for everyone to understand their role in achieving the overall goal and much more likely that everyone will feel ownership over the strategic plan.

It's important that goals be set for everyone in the company and when there are bonuses involved, those bonuses should be tied to those goals. One of the truest sayings in business is, "You get what you pay for." So if you base your bonuses on anything other than the strategic plans you have set to achieve your goals, you won't get what you wanted. It is critical to set goals for each individual, for each supervisor, for each manager, for each vice president based on what they can influence within their area of responsibility.

In the process of developing the tactics and goals, it is very important to avoid the "nice to haves" and the "might as wells." They have a nasty way of creeping into almost every project and of gumming up the works. For us, it was most obvious in the computer area. "We are doing this anyhow, so we might as well . . ." and when we gave in to that kind of thinking, the project usually fell behind schedule and cost far more than budgeted. This was, of course, then promptly explained away by the additional work needed. In the meantime, we were delayed in achieving our basic goals. It is critical to stay focused on the essentials of what are needed to do the job and to avoid the "nice to haves" and the "might as wells." At best, they will delay you and cost you money and at worst they can torpedo the whole project.

Another thing to avoid is the "program of the month" syndrome. All too often, management is too timid in pursuing their strategy. Merits and risks of various alternatives are constantly analyzed and weighed, and different ideas are talked about ad infinitum, none of them strongly acted upon. This sends a terribly mixed message to everyone in the organization.

In my opinion, this "program of the month" syndrome is the result of the thinking of personalities who need to be 120 percent sure that something will work before they get behind it. I have never known any time in business when I was 100 percent sure of anything. If you are a reasonable businessperson and have some feeling for your business and your industry, once you are 70 percent or so sure that something will work, go for it and then make it work. Besides, these 120 percent types have no business being an entrepreneur, anyway. They just don't have the guts to do what it takes to be successful.

Sure, once you get going you will find that you will have to make adjustments because you weren't 100 percent right on every aspect of the plan, but at least you are on your way. There will always be detours, and the "law of unintended consequences" is always in action, but if you keep working at it and making the needed adjustments, you will get to where you need to and where you planned to go, or close to it.

While most of the time we were successful in implementing our strategies, there were times when we weren't. Two were rather costly failures and both failed for the same reason. We didn't put enough of the right resources behind them. And, most critical in my opinion, we weren't willing to stick with it and make it work, and that was a shame. In other words, we tried to ease into them without fully committing ourselves to making them successful.

The first was when we bought a chain of office furniture stores doing a mixture of retail and contract business. We knew nothing about retail (storefront) business but we put one of our Quill people in charge of the operation. The stores weren't doing well when we bought them and there was virtually no management team in place, something we hadn't taken into account. We failed to go out and hire a topflight office furniture management person. I ended up spending a good deal of my time on the project, but I didn't know much about that kind of operation and I couldn't devote the time needed to learn. To make a long story short, we sold the chain and took a big loss on the venture.

The same sort of thing happened when we tried to open a mail order operation in Canada. We sent two of our junior executives to Canada to run the operation. Canada was not an easy market to penetrate. In the first place, it has one-tenth the population of the Unites States, so the potential is limited. That one-tenth is spread out from the Atlantic to the Pacific. Moreover, a portion of Canada is French-speaking Quebec where it is mandatory to use French language literature, so we needed two sets of catalogs or one catalog in two languages. I believe that given time and with the right management, we could have made it work. The Canadians loved our low prices and fast service, but we were losing money and spreading our efforts too thin, so after a few years, we decided to close the operation down.

This kind of failure happens all the time, even on much smaller projects. It really boils down to not putting the right people riding herd on the right project, with enough time available to do the herd riding. If you are trying to do something within your company, such as making your web site a topflight web site, make sure you have a very qualified person who can spend 100 percent of their time on making it happen. We found that when you assign a project like that to someone who has other responsibilities, they always have an excuse for why what you wanted didn't happen. "I was busy with so-and-so or such-and-such," I would always hear. You need to put somebody on top of the project who will live or die with that project.

The lessons we learned were that if you are going to do something, make sure you put the resources behind it to make it happen and give it the time necessary to make it happen.

"The devil is in the details" really applies when it comes to implementing strategy. It's often easy to see, in concept, what should be done, but getting it done is usually a lot tougher. Do you have the right people? If not, will you transfer or fire those who aren't right and find some who are? Some tactics will work and

some will not. Do you have a system for monitoring results of actions quickly so you can make adjustments and changes as necessary? Will top management stay focused on the strategy and
commit the resources needed? Are clearly defined goals set for
everyone in the organization, goals that will lead to the success of
the strategy?

Let me give you one small example. At Quill, our goal was to
ship all orders received by 4 P.M. (later changed to 6 P.M.) the same
day. One day, while walking around the telephone order and order
entry department, I noticed a large stack of papers and asked what
they were. "They're fax orders," someone said. As I looked into
this further, I found that they were letting fax orders go until later
in the day, often into the evening, as they took care of the phone
orders. As a result, orders that came in via fax during the morning
hours often weren't getting entered until sometime in the evening,
too late for the last UPS truck. Thus, we weren't meeting our goal.
But the people in the order entry department thought they were
meeting their goal by entering all orders by the end of the second
shift that day. The strategic goal wasn't interpreted correctly for
the people in this department, so as a result the goal wasn't being
met. They thought *entering* the order the same day was the goal,
while we meant *shipping* the order (in by 6 P.M.) was the goal.

So what we did was to time stamp all incoming fax orders and
set a deadline of entering these orders within 30 minutes of arrival.
A small detail? Yes, but typical of the hundreds and probably thousands of small details that can make your strategy work or fail.
These are the kind of details that have to be looked after day after
day. Because in business, not only is the "devil in the details" but
so are success and profits.

This brings me to another very important concept for running
a good business and for making your strategy work: do the simple
things well because almost everything is simple. Let me explain.

Take a marketing sales program as an example. A group of people from marketing, sales, and advertising meet to begin mapping
out the program. Studies are made. Plans are drawn up. Advertising

literature is prepared with many people making sure the artwork is just so, that the copy is hard hitting, that the offer is presented right. Money, effort, and sweat are put into developing the program, but it doesn't produce the long-term results hoped for. Why?

It could be that the program wasn't good in the first place. Or perhaps it was good but some of the simple things were not done well. Maybe the premium offered wasn't ordered in time and wasn't available when the program hit because someone didn't notify the purchasing department in time to order and receive the premium.

Or perhaps provisions weren't made to handle the increased order volume and the phones weren't answered promptly. Customers got put on hold for a long time and kept receiving that now familiar recorded message, "Your business is important to us. Our agents are busy serving other customers, and so on."

Simple things that are not done well aggravate and lose customers, turn off prospective customers, and waste a lot of money. And simple things not done well can frustrate your own employees when the best laid plans of mice, men, and entrepreneurs go awry because the simple things that can make a big idea work weren't taken care of.

The shame of this is that it never has to be that way. In truth, almost everything *is* simple. Most things in business and in life are not brain surgery. They simply need the proper attention and effort to make them happen. When they don't happen or don't happen well, it is usually because no one in the organization thought they were important enough to make sure that they did happen and happen well. This leads me to another important lesson for every business leader. To you, simple things will often seem obvious. You will often feel you don't need to verbalize them because they are so obvious. You might think you don't want to offend your people because, well, it is just so obvious. *Say the obvious.* Make sure everybody knows that the simplest things must get done and that you are paying attention to those simple things.

Too often, the president of a company (and all things do start from the top) or the marketing manager or the customer service manager or the warehouse manager simply doesn't feel strongly enough about the importance of the small, simple things to make sure that they do, indeed, happen well. This is nothing new, but it can spell disaster because one simple thing not attended to can lead to a chain reaction of multiple simple things not attended to leading to a grand idea failing.

I have no doubt that the cultures of most successful companies include a strong focus on making sure that the simple things are done well and that the leadership of those companies understand that most things are also that simple. (I have a sign in my office, even today, that reads IT IS TOO THAT SIMPLE, which I had made because after I suggested something people would often say, "It's not that simple."

It's important to turn everything possible into routine processes (and this includes far more things than most people think) and then keep improving the routine. It's important to make sure that everyone down to the newest person at the lowest level knows exactly what their responsibilities are. Constant monitoring and correcting are always necessary to make sure that all those simple things are, indeed, done well.

I believe that success depends more on doing the simple things well than it does on coming up with grand and eloquent plans and programs. Even in a very small business, let's say a plumbing business, success depends as much or more on showing up when promised, doing a neat job, and cleaning up afterward as it does on any advertising or promotional efforts. Probably more so, since word of mouth is the best advertising a small business can have.

Having a well defined mission and a good strategy are important to achieving success. Implementing them well is what matters most. Yet this is where far too many companies fall down. It is a shame that this happens because for the most part *It is, too, that simple!*

# Chapter 12

# Forecasting and Budgeting

"It's hard to make predictions, especially about the future." Make sure to keep that in mind when you start making forecasts and when you do your budgeting. Most bankers surely keep this in mind when asked to make loans based on forecasts and budgets. Because all too often forecasts and budgets are really nothing more than wishful thinking, nothing more than "pie in the sky" assumptions. Very often they are based on that old song, "Accentuate the positive, eliminate the negative."

In my opinion and based on my own experience, you shouldn't even believe your own forecasts, at least not to the point that you totally base your budgeting on them. Your budgeting should actually be based on the idea that your forecasts probably won't be right, because if they're not it's very easy to budget yourself into trouble.

How many ways can you get into trouble with forecasting? Oh, if I could count the ways. Elbert Hubbard, a business writer and business philosopher in the late nineteenth and early twentieth century pointed out one way when he wrote, "Forecast: To observe that which has passed and guess it will happen again." Many forecasts, including many in the public sector, are based on this "straight line" style of forecasting. Just think of how our federal budget surpluses were being forecast in the late 1990s, with the assumption of ever-increasing revenues. And then along came the recession. Business-people fall into the same trap. They forget that things change. You lose a major customer. The economy goes south. Your major customer runs into trouble and buys a lot less, or the whole industry runs into trouble. A new, very aggressive competitor suddenly appears. On and on the unpredicted possibilities go.

There is no question that you absolutely must look at your past performance to begin to project your future performance. But you have to look at it with a very critical eye. Were there some extraordinary events, good or bad, that made your past year(s) better or worse than would otherwise have been expected? What were these factors and are they going to continue? What are you planning to do in the future that will affect your performance? Here you must be very careful not to assume too great a result from some of your new initiatives. Even if they are very good initiatives, it usually takes longer than you might think for them to show the hoped for results; thus, to build all of those hoped for results into your budget too soon could be a costly mistake. Looking at the past and using it as a guide to the future is one important component of your forecasting. But it is only one of several.

Another way you can go wrong is, as someone once put it, "imagining that which has never (or very rarely) happened before is really going to happen." This is even a more dangerous threat than straight line forecasting. It is a very common mistake businesspeople make. It is a particularly common problem in start-up companies. A lot of investor money has been lost because of this kind of rosy forecasting.

With those dangers in mind, it is nevertheless very important to perform forecasts and then to create budgets even if not immediately implemented (which is probably a good idea) cautiously based on those forecasts. Used properly they can be important business tools. For example, they could easily and quickly show whether a proposed course of action, even if everything went according to plan (which it seldom does), would produce satisfactory bottom line results. Also, budgets and forecasts can be good disciplinary tools in terms of setting goals to be achieved and restraints on how much can be spent.

A good forecasting and budgeting system allows you to see a year in advance what the likely results will be based on what you are planning to do. Then, if you don't like those results, you can plan on how you will change them, cutting certain expenses, going after more volume, and so on. It is sort of like building a new house. It's a lot easier and cheaper to make changes during the planning process than it is to make them after the house is under construction or already built.

Also planning forces you to think about your business at a higher level than just solving the daily problems as they come up. Planning forces you to pull away from the day-to-day issues that, while important, can consume you completely. It forces you to look ahead and to set up plans and controls. It gives you a road map to follow. Projecting and budgeting, in my opinion, is a critical element for the success of any endeavor, large or small.

So how can you use forecasts and budgets to help run your business? Don't do a single forecast and budget. Do at least three. One would be what you really, honestly believe will happen. Then there should be another that is a bit more optimistic, sort of a stretch goal. And the third should be one that is *much* more conservative, a worst case scenario. Then use the much more conservative forecast and budget when making commitments that are going to cost money, particularly for major, long-term fixed costs.

Then use all three when setting bonus goals. The middle forecast, the one you really, honestly believe will happen, should be your "target" bonus goal. The more optimistic one, your "stretch" bonus goal, and the much more conservative one should be your minimum bonus goal. By the way, if you really want buy-in from your people, all your managers on up should be involved in the process of forecasting and budgeting, and they should each involve a few key people.

At Quill, my brothers and I along with a few key people would develop a game plan for the next year. For example, we might be willing to sacrifice some profit for a faster growth in sales. Or we might feel that we wanted to sacrifice some growth in the interest of better profits. We set the overall direction for the coming year.

From there, we met with all the department managers, who then involved their supervisors and others they felt could help. Merchandising and marketing, for example, would focus on sales and gross profit goals. Then, from those sales projections, each department developed their budgets. How many additional people would they need? How could they handle the added volume more efficiently? What new, or better, systems would they need? What capital investments?

At numerous meetings, with one another, with the vice presidents, and with the financial person in charge of the whole process, assumptions and numbers were challenged and changes were made. Then the financial people put together the projected profit and loss budgets, capital expenditures, and cash flow budgets. Then, if the bottom line didn't come out as desired, more work was done: a little cutting here, a little more investment there, and so on.

Then we sat down with top management for a final, very thorough review, looking at it line by line, approving, questioning, and making suggestions. In the end we arrived at numbers we could all live with, numbers we all believed in. Everyone's profit sharing and bonuses would be based on these numbers, so it was important that all had a hand in creating the goals. Most importantly, it is vital that the folks responsible for making the numbers believed in the budget and believed that it was "their" budget so that they would fight to make it happen.

The numbers we used in budgeting, for example inventory turnover, accounts receivable as a percent of sales, bad debt losses, and so on were numbers we used from our own experience and how we thought we could improve on that past performance. While we looked at the "industry averages" published by the association, we always expected to do much better, and we did.

While the industry average for inventory turns was somewhere near four turns a year, ours approached 10 a year. And while on average, bad debt losses were somewhere near 2 percent a year, ours was one-half of 1 percent, and so on.

Averages are interesting but meaningless. One of my favorite sayings that I repeated many times in various conversations with our people was about the man who drowned walking across a river that was an *average* of three feet deep. I never wanted our people to feel they were doing well if they equaled the average. We had to beat it and beat it by a wide margin. Otherwise we were just a mixture of some good and some bad.

As an aside here, let me comment on something we learned along the way. For years we kept our financial results as a closely held secret. Just my brothers and I knew what they were. Then, gradually as we grew we began to share these results with one or two other top people in the organization. Then we shared them with all the officers and managers in the company. In the end, we had monthly meetings with about 25 of our people who were privy to all the numbers.

Most entrepreneurs are afraid to share the bottom line results, and even some other numbers with others in their organization. They fear that others, once they know the numbers, might want bigger salaries or bigger bonuses. And then there is just the general fear of sharing the numbers.

But after years of sharing the numbers with many others in the organization, I can't imagine not sharing them. Forecasting and budgeting would be impossible and meaningless if they weren't shared. Also, the troops might suspect that the owners aren't being fair in the contribution to profit sharing or in the bonuses if they didn't know that vice presidents and managers were looking at the numbers. In publicly held companies, these numbers are there for the whole world to see. In privately held companies they too often are guarded more closely than the queen's jewels, to the detriment of the company.

Then, most importantly, don't just look at the numbers at the beginning of the year and then put them into a drawer and forget about them. Actual sales results should be measured *every day*, not only against last year but also against your forecasts. Then, every month with your key people, spend several hours going over your monthly financial statement, line by line, measuring it against last year and against your forecasts and budgets.

Based on the trends you see, then create a new forecast for the remainder of the year, adjusted up or down according to what is happening and why it is happening. Based on these new forecasts, look at your budgets and determine what adjustments are needed in order to make sure you maximize your bottom line results. By proceeding this way, you are constantly making those needed adjustments on a timely basis as you go through the year instead of looking only at a year-end statement and wondering why you didn't do better. You also catch and correct, or capitalize on, trends very quickly.

Frankly, I favor *not* making long-term, hard to rescind, financial, and other resource commitments needed to handle optimistic or even target projections until you actually know that you are hitting those projections. Short of hurting customer service, it is better to pay higher costs on a temporary basis, if you are doing better than the minimum target budgeted for, than to commit to costs that are hard to change if goals aren't met.

If you really do make or exceed that minimum projection, the higher, temporary cost of overtime, temporary labor, or outsourcing is easier to absorb than the higher cost of a more fixed commitment would be if you don't hit your targets. It is a better business decision to pay higher shipping and restocking costs for more frequent shipments if you are exceeding your minimum projections than it would be to pay a long-term lease commitment if you miss your projections. At Quill, for example, in the late 1970s, we ran out of both warehouse and office space because we were growing far faster than expected. By the time we were able to build a new facility, we were operating out of four warehouse spaces and three office spaces in the industrial park we were in. Was it inefficient? Sure! But we made good profits for the four years we had to operate that way. And I have seen a lot of companies do it the other way and lose money. See the chapter "How to Do Almost Everything Wrong."

As a final comment on forecasting and budgeting, I want to make clear that they are very valuable management tools when used properly, but you must be careful not to forecast yourself into trouble. It's very easy to do because most entrepreneurs are optimistic by nature. I think the best way to look at budgeting and forecasting is to, as many have said, "Hope for the best and prepare for the worst."

# Chapter 13

# Using Your Financial Statements to Get Where You Want to Go

Global positioning systems (GPS) in cars are a great way to get where you want to go. Enter your destination and whether you want the fastest route, the no-highway route, or the shortest route and the system directs you, turn by turn, how to get there. Your monthly financial statements should be the GPS for your business. Combined with an annual projection and monthly, updated, forecasts, they are your road map and your early warning system when you have made a wrong turn. Without them you are flying blind and you can get way off course before you realize that you are headed in the wrong direction.

Sadly, many entrepreneurs don't use projections, forecasts, and financial statements that way. Some don't even get a detailed monthly financial statement, just an annual statement. And all too often entrepreneurs just look at the bottom line to see whether they made a profit and how much it was and then throw the financial statement into a drawer. What a waste of a valuable tool.

Accept that generally, as soon as you make an annual projection, it begins to go wrong. And why wouldn't it? If you looked on a map and found the road you wanted to take to get to your destination and then, when you got on that road, you locked your steering wheel in place, you would soon find yourself off the road and in a ditch or, worse yet, smashed into a telephone pole.

To get where you're going, as you travel on a particular road, you must make minor adjustments as you go along. And, when you get to some bad spots in your route, you have to make definite changes in direction. In the car, a GPS system can help you make the major changes and your own awareness helps you make the minor adjustments.

With a business, the annual projection plots your course, what you expect the results will be from the actions you plan to take. But right from the start you know the projection is not going to be totally accurate. That's where your monthly financial statement review comes in. A monthly financial statement, properly prepared and reviewed in detail, line by line, allows you to see, at short intervals, how the company is doing. This, in turn, allows you to make minor (and some big) adjustments quickly before there is a major problem.

Financial statements show more than just profits and losses. They expose every area of your business to scrutiny to see if each is performing as expected. The way to determine that is to compare each line item with your projections and with last year. You compare your actual numbers, line per line, with your assumptions on your projections. And then it is critical to ask yourself, and discuss with your other top people why there is a variance, good or bad. By the way, each month after you compare your monthly financial statement with your projection, you should reforecast for the rest of the year based on what you have learned and what you plan to do.

Here's how we did it at Quill. Within 10 days (no later) after the end of the month, we had a review of our financial statements (which ran to more than 25 pages). My brothers and I, our chief financial officer, and about 25 of our top people, would spend a minimum of four hours reviewing the statements line by line. The group included the heads of each area of the company, from human resources, merchandising, marketing, operations, computer systems, credit, accounting, and so on, plus a few other key people.

As I've mentioned and I want to repeat, one of the mistakes many entrepreneurs make is in not sharing their numbers with others in the company. We were like that for many years, keeping our numbers a secret from the very people responsible for achieving the right numbers.

Sharing the numbers with your top people has advantages. Chief among them is that it gives them a read on how they are doing, how their department is performing. It shows them what they have to do. It helps give them a basis for helping prepare future budgets. It also gives them an opportunity to see what is happening in the rest of the company, where they may have some ideas on how to make improvements.

In any event, we went over the profit and loss statement line by line. Our sales, as compared with last year and with this year's projections, were the first item we looked at. Then, our gross profit as a percent of sales was next. Was it holding steady, heading up or heading down? If up or down, there was a discussion as to why. The same went for every line item on our statement, overall and by department (particularly in the area of personnel costs). We paid extra attention to the items our financial people had highlighted as they prepared the document.

We carefully scrutinized the balance sheet. Were our accounts receivables at the target we had set? Our terms were net 30 days and if open receivables went over 35 days, that was a warning signal that we weren't doing something right, and our credit manager had to explain what was going on.

Inventory turns was also a critical number. The slower the turns, the more money we had to have invested in inventory, not to mention the more space needed to hold that larger inventory. While the industry average of inventory turns was four or five turns a year, our target was 10 turns (how many times our inventory completely turns over, as if the whole warehouse would be emptied and restocked). We were doing that virtually every month. Of course, some items turned more slowly and others more quickly, but on average we were getting our 10 turns. If our turns were less than our target, we wanted to know why and we wanted the situation corrected.

As I have said before, I was always sensitive to the concept of "averages." For example, if someone spoke about an average order size of $200 this year versus $175 last year, that was good only for tracking a trend that might indicate something, such as getting more very large orders. Or it could mean that order sizes overall were going up. The numbers needed digging into if you really wanted to know what was going on with your business.

Receivables turns are important because the quicker you collect your money from your customers, the less money you need to invest there. And the same is true with inventory turns. If you could turn your inventory fast enough, you could actually sell the merchandise before you had to pay for it. It always amazes me about how lax many businesspeople are about things like this, which result in their having to keep going to the bank for loans (and thus adding another expense—interest—to their financial statements).

The faster you collect your money and turn your inventory, the more prompt-pay cash discounts you can take on what you purchase, and the more money you have for advertising and marketing, to build your business or for improvements in your computer systems, and for all the other areas that help you grow your business faster and run it better.

Also, we were careful to make sure that our current assets were in the right ratio to our current liabilities so we knew we weren't headed for problems in that area. A one to one ratio is considered good, but we tried to maintain a two to one ratio, meaning we had twice as much in assets that could be turned into cash quickly to pay off the current debts, such as our accounts payable, which were due soon.

We never left these meetings totally satisfied with what the statements showed. While the sales and the bottom line profits may have been good, there were always ways in which some areas could have been better and we would immediately begin to work on them.

Some entrepreneurs feel that "bean counting" is not a part of entrepreneuring. But they couldn't be more wrong. If you don't count the beans, frequently and carefully, there may not be any beans to count, or at least fewer of them than there could have been.

Yes, a careful review of the monthly financial statements helps keep you on track toward your goals. But you must make sure not to accept any excuses or rationalizations to explain away deviations from your expectations. You must be fiercely determined to meet those expectations. If you are not meeting them, then you should reexamine your expectations and determine whether they are realistic. If you decide they are realistic, then you have to get busy finding out why you aren't meeting those expectations. You can't bank excuses.

Yes, your monthly financial statements truly are your GPS system for your business. You should pay very close attention to them. They will pay handsome dividends.

## Chapter 14

# You Can, Too, Argue with Success!

Some say you can't argue with success. Well, I guess if you never want to get bigger and better or even, perhaps, to stay in business, that may be right. All too often, people say that just to close off discussion of how something can be done better. People think it so they can avoid the hard, but profitable, work of finding ways to be even better. The fact of the matter is that you can *and you should* "argue with success."

Last year was a great year. You made a $1,000,000 profit. How can you argue with that?

I'll bet that you could argue with that success. I would bet that if you tore apart what went on, you might discover that you really had made $1,500,000 or more but had thrown away $500,000 through waste and errors, by selling to certain unprofitable accounts, or as a result of poor pricing or bad buying or just a lot of waste in the operation.

On top of all that, you might have made a lot more money by focusing on some opportunities that you simply overlooked or were too busy to take advantage of. Or maybe you weren't aggressive enough in your marketing, your selling, your pricing, or your costs.

You should always argue with and challenge success. And the time to do it *is* when you are successful, when you have the luxury of time and resources to become even more successful. But most people don't begin to look for the opportunities to find all the waste that is draining away earnings, to aggressively look for ways to improve their products or services, or to more aggressively increase business until they are forced to by the threat of losses or possibility of bankruptcy. By then, it's usually too late. I often relate the story about how I eventually learned the lesson of 85/15—that usually just 15 percent of what a CEO does is what a CEO ought to be doing. One of those things every CEO should be doing is focusing on aggressively finding more business, improving their products and service, and weeding out waste.

Examples of not doing this are legendary. The American auto industry is a major example. They were satisfied with their long-standing leadership position and were content to just bend steel in different forms year after year. But then the Japanese and the Germans practically stole the market from them before they began to wake up. Montgomery Ward is out of business and Sears lags badly in the retail market while Target and Wal-Mart now rule the roost. And I suppose someday someone will come along with some new way of marketing products, and then they will be left behind.

There's a process called "creative destruction" that sums it up pretty well. While you are successful with what you are doing, you should always be looking for better ways of doing it so that you are the one who is that next big success, not some competitor. Use past success to find new, greater success.

A very common and dangerous attitude to have in business is to become satisfied with your success. When you do, you begin to set yourself up for stagnation, at best, and decline and failure at worst.

When it comes to costs, for example, as I've said before, far too many businesses are like leaky pails with hundreds of very small holes, where far too much of what is put into them leaks out. Plugging those leaks is an unending task because there are always new leaks that begin to take effect. And it isn't a one man job. It's a job that takes everyone in the organization to do effectively. But it is usually one person's job to create the drive to find all those leaks and to plug them. That person, of course, is you.

At Quill, we thought we were running a pretty efficient company. But after the industry changed and we decided we had to be competitive with the superstores, we cut our selling prices so much that our gross profit margin went down nine full points, from

44 percent to 35 percent. As a result we weren't making any money and were forced to find savings. We talked to everyone in the company and looked in every nook and cranny to find savings big and small. Within a year we found enough savings to put us back into the black. Increased sales and continued pressure on reducing costs rebuilt our profits to previous levels and beyond.

Also, as I have mentioned before, these savings ranged from such small things as going to longer-lasting bulbs in the exit signs so we had to change bulbs less often (a savings of about $5,000 per year) all the way on up to major systems changes, such as buying equipment that would allow us to process incoming checks (which were in the many thousands every day) in-house instead of having the bank do that. That resulted in major savings and led to a day's savings in getting credited with the deposits earlier, which increased our interest income. Then, of course, there was the always reliable push to get better discounts and more advertising support from our vendors.

All of those savings were found in what we and almost everyone else felt was an already very well run company.

More recently I had, and am having as I write this a similar experience with Successories, which just about everyone agrees was a very poorly run company. It was a totally unfocused company with delusions of grandeur that had led to many unwise decisions. We tried to sell the company, but only one group offered to buy it, and then only if I agreed to stay in and keep my money in. There was no way I or my brothers, when I asked them, felt that I could work with outside partners, and I couldn't see where they would be bringing very much to the party, anyway. Every dollar they were going to put into the company they intended to borrow. That meant that they would want to drag profits out of the company as quickly as they became available in order to pay down their debt. Ah, the workings of the modern entrepreneurial mind.

But in any event I decided to buy the company myself to protect, if possible, my investment along with the investments of a few others who had put some money in along with me a few years earlier. Besides, I really don't like the stock market and it felt good to own another honest-to-goodness company, even if it was losing money, big time.

Once I had announced that I was putting in a bid to buy the company, and months before the Securities and Exchange Commission had approved the purchase, we brought together everyone in the company so I could talk with all of them at once.

Now, this was a great group of people, folks who had been through an awful lot over the past 10 years, with always disappointing sales and losses, with few, and sometimes no, pay raises and certainly no bonuses. The attitude at the top had been, "Don't give me any suggestions. You are being paid to work and we are being paid to think." Or at least that was the gist of it. But in spite of all that they loved the company and believed in its products.

My message to everyone was simple. This is a great company, with great products and a terrific work force. If we are to survive and you are to keep your jobs, we must cut out every penny of waste. I promised them that no one would lose their job as a result of efficiencies they found, even if they recommended eliminating their own position. If they did that, we would find them other work. I told them that people would lose their jobs if they were lazy, if they were troublemakers, if they did a poor job. I also told them that I was putting a good deal of money into the company so it would be solvent and could aggressively pursue growth. But I told them, "We need your input, your ideas on how to save money and on how to do things better. You are the folks actually doing the work, and you know better than anyone else where money is being wasted." I went on to tell them that we would not jeopardize customer service in order to save money. In fact, while saving money, I also wanted to improve both the quality of the product and our customer service.

As of the time I am writing this, we have shrunk the company by cutting out its money losing retail chain of stores and more and have found in excess of $4,000,000 in savings in a company that was $30,000,000 (and now is somewhat smaller). And the savings are still coming in, with hardly a week passing without some new savings being found. And we are now profitable.

At both Quill and Successories, most of the savings were found by people doing the work. We led the charge, with constant reminders on the walls, in meetings, at every opportunity. We had awards and recognition and thank-you programs. We focused folks on looking for savings, not just doing their daily work. They did the rest, big time.

All of those savings, both at Quill and at Successories, were there to be found *before* we were forced to find them. After we found all those savings at Quill, my brothers and I kept saying to ourselves, "My God, look how much more money we could have made before and, just as importantly, how much more competitive we could have been in our pricing and promotions and how much faster we could have grown." Of course, for us at Quill it was like crying while on your way to the bank. But at Successories it was an absolute necessity or the company, even with my additional funding, was heading for bankruptcy.

The point is that in both cases, we should have found those saving and those new ways of doing things *before* we were forced to. We should have been challenging ourselves and everyone else in the company to constantly be looking for better and less expensive ways of doing things. Frankly, at Quill we thought we were trying to run a very efficient company. Compared to most companies out there, we were a model of efficiency. But we found out that we were far from being as efficient as we were capable of being. Even after we rebuilt our profitability through all those savings, there were more to be found and today there are probably still more.

At Quill, we were successful and continually trying to improve. Our problem there was that we really were successful, one of the largest in the country in our industry and nicely profitable. As a result, we were guilty of not arguing enough with our success, not challenging ourselves enough, until we were forced to. I'll never make that mistake again. Now that Successories is actually making money, we are going to keep the pressure on to find more and more ways to save money and to improve on how we do things, including taking a very hard look at our basic business model, which hasn't worked very well over the years.

For every entrepreneur from the smallest to the largest, all of this should be a day in and day out effort involving every single person in the company. Find ways to cut costs! But never sacrifice quality or service. In fact, while looking for those cost savings, always look for ways to *improve* quality and customer service. We found that the search for cost savings almost always turned up ways to improve on what we were doing.

Just as importantly, always look for ways to improve your business model. Always be careful, as my late father-in-law used to say, to "not throw out the baby with the bath water," but always be looking at every aspect of your business to try to improve it. If you don't, there are a lot of competitors out there who will do it for you or to you.

Perhaps the best philosophy to have is expressed in a desk sign one of my daughters gave me because of my constant use of the words, "That's great, but . . . " The sign reads WE'RE HAPPY BUT NOT SATISFIED.

That's not a bad attitude to have. In fact, I think it's a great attitude to have, in business and in life.

# Chapter 15

# Building a Great Corporate Culture

A corporate culture can just happen—or you can make it happen.

When I founded Quill, my vision was nothing as grand as what finally happened. But I knew I wanted to be in business for myself and that somehow I could make it work. Later, when my brothers joined me, we all had the same values of hard work, high integrity, doing the best job it was possible to do, being fair with our employees, and serving our customers extraordinarily well. This was how we lived our lives and this became the basis of our company culture.

We constantly worked to do all of those things better and better. And as we continued to grow, we built on those beliefs by constantly talking about them with our people at every opportunity.

This chapter tells how we built that culture, and my hope is that it will give you some ideas on how you can do the same. I believe that a clearly defined mission and a strong corporate culture (backed by a lot of hard work) will lead to great success. It did for us, and it can for you. But don't just let it happen. Make it happen!

Companies, like people, have unique personalities that include integrity (or a lack thereof), an individual way of doing things, and a particular way of responding to competition and to customers. In other words, companies have a culture. The crucial decision in any organization is whether the culture evolves on its own, or whether it is carefully developed to drive a company to great success.

Either way, once strongly established, as all cultures become over time, it directs the way things are done throughout the company and is one of the strongest drivers of success, failure, or just plain mediocrity in your organization.

The culture of a company will dictate how a company commits its assets, how it responds to challenges and opportunities, what kind of people are hired, what kind are promoted, what kind are fired, and so much more. The culture of a company is the most powerful driving force within that company, just as it is with individuals and with nations. Think of the importance of the culture embodied within the Declaration of Independence and the Constitution, and what effect that has had on how the United States has evolved. Culture is much too important a factor to just let happen.

So you must think long and hard about what kind of culture you want and what kind of culture will help drive your company toward the goals you want to achieve. Once established, there will be some core ideas in your culture that should never change, but there will be other elements of the culture that may adapt over time in response to competition and to customer needs and desires. For example, as their customers' understanding of technology increased, IBM changed their culture from that of focusing on "what we make" to focusing on "what the customers need."

As with almost everything else that goes into building a strong, profitable, good company, building the kind of culture that will make all that happen is not some strange, exotic art nor does it require some special genius. But, as with almost everything else in building a good company, it does require a lot of thought and effort to build the right culture and then a lot of hard work each and every day to reinforce it.

It starts at the top. The old saying that "Actions speak louder than words" certainly applies when it comes to corporate culture. The people at the head of the company can talk all they want about honesty, customer service, and hard work, but if their actions every single day don't match their words, no one in the company will be fooled for long, if at all. Every action taken by a supervisor, a manager, a vice president, or the president will reinforce the *true* culture of the company, regardless of what is written in the company handbooks or talked about at company meetings. As usual, nothing speaks louder than actions. And those actions start at the top and trickle down through the other layers of management to the entire company.

For example, in far too many cases, the president will talk about the importance of good customer service and building employee loyalty. But at the same time, the focus is directly on the bottom line to the exclusion of almost everything else, and the very strong message that goes out to everyone is to "cut costs." Cutting costs, without the consideration of the impact on the improvement in good customer service or building employee loyalty, becomes the focus of most meetings and most conversations—and the basis of most rewards.

In such a company, if a manager or employee is faced with a choice between cutting costs or improving customer service, they will almost always choose cutting costs, even to the detriment of customer service.

By the same token, if the top person doesn't work hard, it isn't long before others in the company aren't working hard, either. If the president is a screamer and faultfinder, others in the company soon will become the same.

On the other hand, when management, through their actions, reinforces the kind of culture they want, employees will respond by embracing that culture. And those who don't are soon out of the company, by their own choice or otherwise. So the good news is that you can create the kind of culture in your company that will drive it to great success.

You need to start with a mission. The single most important purpose for a strong culture is to carry out the mission of the organization. Lawrence J. Peter had it exactly right. "If you don't know where you are going, you will probably end up somewhere else."

But when you have a clearly defined mission, a very focused culture will result in specific actions designed to carry out that mission. Let me give you a few examples.

*The Quill Mission Statement:* "By giving our customers uncompromisingly outstanding satisfaction, by being a great marketer of products to business and by operating at the highest degree of efficiency, we will achieve significant growth in sales and in profitability."

We worked hard and long in crafting that mission statement, choosing (and changing) each word to get exactly what we wanted. In the end, we had a mission statement that became the foundation for almost everything we did and for our culture.

Let's take a closer look at how this mission statement helped to define our company. "Uncompromising, outstanding customer service" headed the list. It was of critical importance that we put the customer first. Then, "being a great marketer" said that we are a marketing and distribution company and our goal is to be great, not just okay. "To business customers" meant that we would not try to market or sell to individuals. "By operating at the highest degree of efficiency" meant that we would constantly look for ways to become more and more efficient while still giving that "uncompromising, outstanding customer service."

We believed that with this combination of words and ideas, growth in sales and profitability would become a part of the process. In other words we were telling our people that by doing the right things in the right ways sales and profit growth would happen. We also wanted everyone to take pride in their company. Working at Quill wasn't just a job, it really was a mission, one they could believe in.

The people at Quill did take great pride in the extraordinary service we gave, in finding ways to be more efficient and in constantly becoming better at both of those objectives through the constant training we provided them. Our motto for all of us (you might even call it a mantra because we constantly repeated it) was, "Become the best you are capable of being."

Here is another mission statement I would like to share with you because it has been so effective in taking kids from some of the poorest neighborhoods in Chicago and qualifying 100 percent of them to go on to the top universities in the country. It is the mission statement of Providence St. Mel, a private school run by a unique individual, Paul Adams.

The students recite this mission, or "pledge," aloud and in unison, each and every morning:

At Providence St. Mel, we believe . . .
We believe in the creation of inspired lives
produced by the miracle of hard work.
We are not frightened by the challenges of reality,
but believe that we can change our conception
of this world and our place within it.
So, we work, plan, build and dream in that order.
We believe that one must earn the right to dream.
Our talent, discipline and integrity will be
our contribution to a new world.
Because we believe that we can take this place,
this time, and this people,
and make a better place,
a better time and a better people.

With God's help, we find a way or make one.

This powerful mission statement, repeated aloud and together each morning, has had an amazing effect on thousands of young children. It is a powerful mission statement that clearly sets forth what they want these young people to do as well as the strategies to achieve those goals. When you visit the school you see how this mission is carried out in the culture that's so evident.

Paul wants to change the concept that these poor and disadvantaged kids have of the world. And he wants to change their conception of their place within that world. In other words, he wants these kids to actively know that they can become educated, successful leaders in the world. Or, in the somewhat simpler words of a sergeant in a movie I once saw, "Not having is no excuse for not getting."

If you can develop a mission as short, direct, and powerful as this, and keep repeating it so that everyone knows it and believes it, the whole organization will pull together as one to make it happen. Believe me, a strong, well-thought-out mission statement focuses everyone, much like the rays of the sun are focused through a magnifying glass on one spot, with a very powerful effect.

In developing and reinforcing a corporate culture, there are certain rules that you must follow to be successful. Not just give lip service to, but really live by, just as there are certain rules in developing a civilized society or in any other human endeavor. Without such rules, the culture becomes just so many words on paper, with no real meaning and no real impact on the results the organization is trying to achieve.

*Rules to Live By*
Here are a few of the rules that we developed at Quill.

1. *It is important to set standards (moral, ethical, performance, customer service, and more) and then live up to them.* Small infractions soon destroy all. As the new century unfolds, the newspapers are filled with the scandals in the mutual fund industry and the stories of corporate malfeasance by top executives. It will take a long time to rebuild the trust the American people have had in these organizations.

2. *You must internalize!* Those standards and your total mission statement must become a part of your everyday life, part of the everyday life of your company. Make your mission statement part of every conversation in one way or another. Use success and failure stories to illustrate certain points. Give examples of what did happen and what could have happened, always being careful to give great praise where warranted and to not criticize in public. Find every way possible to get the message across; in company newsletters, at meetings, in casual conversations, even on shipping cartons, packing slips, and invoices. Remember, while you are communicating to customers, you are also communicating to employees. And don't be afraid to make promises. It becomes a source of pride to your people.

3. *Give people freedom—but!* The "but" is that they have freedom to act, within the goals and standards you have set for the company. If there is to be a deviation from those goals and standards, it must be discussed thoroughly and a conscious decision made by management to actually change the goals and standards, or at least to test making a change. Without this ability and willingness to change, the company could be locked into a mission statement that no longer responds to a changing market. But as with amendments to the U.S. Constitution, such amendments should not be easy to make.

4. *You cannot lie to your people.* If you do not wholeheartedly believe in the culture you are trying to create and implant into your organization, then don't even try. Your insincerity will be obvious to your employees as well as to your customers. It would be better to go with what you really believe and hope that is good enough.

Core values drive how you and your people act and react. Every society, every organization, every individual has a set of values, good or bad, that drives their every action, values against which they measure their own actions. Early in our country's history, the values of the freedom of the individual, of the sanctity of private property, and of the importance of the free marketplace were clearly stated and incorporated into the Declaration of Independence and into the Constitution. They became the touchstones against which we measured our actions as a nation. They codified the culture of our country.

Core values are a very strong component of your company's corporate culture. *Every human endeavor is guided, shaped, and supported by basic underlying values that are the foundation for every decision and every action.* Let me share with you the core values that we articulated and reinforced into the Quill culture over the years. They served us well.

These values, when known and properly understood, gave everyone in the Quill organization the freedom and ability to treat customers, fellow workers, vendors, and the community in the Quill way. They also clearly define the characteristics of the individuals who will be happiest and most successful as part of the Quill adventure. Make no mistake about it, not every individual fits into any particular culture. Many times we found that certain individuals did not fit into the Quill culture. The sooner it is recognized and acted upon, the better it is for the company and the individual. As Vince Lombardi said, there is "strength to be derived by unity."

## The Quill Values

### Value #1 Uncompromisingly Outstanding Customer Satisfaction

At Quill there is, and must be, a passion for satisfying our customers. We must be uncompromising in meeting and exceeding our promises and our customers' expectations.

Customers must receive everything they expect—and more—the first time and on each contact with us. But, when there is a problem, we must make extraordinary efforts to ensure the problem is resolved quickly, correctly, and to the customers' total satisfaction on the very first attempt.

*This core value, instilled in every person at Quill, encourages passion for providing uncompromising customer satisfaction.*

### Value #2 Continual Learning

At Quill, our goal is to help all individuals become the best they are capable of being so, in turn, they can help Quill become the best it is capable of being. Many companies say that "people are our most important asset." At Quill our goal is to make that a reality by providing the training and educational opportunities and a working environment that helps each individual become the very best he or she can be.

There are constant changes in the marketplace, in technology, and in customer expectations. Also, each of us has different levels of knowledge and ability, and all must constantly strive to raise those levels.

Each employee is expected to make the commitment and effort (in some cases on their own time) to take advantage of learning opportunities. Progress in this effort will be an important element in success at Quill.

*This core value provides all employees with the training, the tools, and the appropriate authority they need to succeed.*

### Value #3 A Hard Work Ethic

We believe strongly in the value of hard work. It is only through intelligent hard work that each individual within the company can make a difference—in his or her own success and in Quill's.

So we expect a lot from everyone at Quill. In return, we help each individual become the very best he or she is capable of being.

At the same time while hard work is the norm at Quill, we can also have fun at work; experiencing the excitement of challenges, the satisfaction of achievement, the pride of personal growth, and the thrill of winning.

Hard, consistent effort and pride in our achievements can make this happen.

*This core value constantly reinforces the concept that just being "good" is not good enough. We must be outstanding.*

### Value #4 Enabling People

All individuals in the company should be enabled to do their job as it should be done in order to reach their goals and for the company to reach its goals. Risk taking and trust are the critical elements that are important to the success of this idea.

Each individual will be encouraged to take ownership of his or her job and is encouraged to constantly come up with ideas for improvement. Quill provides the training and gives everyone the appropriate authority to make decisions and to act to carry out his or her job.

*This core value continually raises the standards of performance, and we were always looking for new ways to provide our customers with outstanding satisfaction.*

The job is never done. There are always new and better ways for serving customers, particularly because of the new technology that keeps coming out.

It is amazing how people, given the encouragement and opportunity, can come up with great ways to serve the customer better, and along the way save money while doing it.

## Value #5 Teamwork

At Quill, we believe that true teamwork will enhance both individual and corporate performance.

When individuals have the opportunity to combine their talents and knowledge in the quest for solutions and improvements, they produce much better results. They also learn from the experience and broaden their knowledge and abilities.

At Quill, we encourage teamwork in every area of the company. In seeking improvements as well as in problem solving, we use the team concept within departments, between departments, and across the whole company. We also extend this concept in working with our suppliers in "partnering" relationships.

This core value

- Encourages and recognizes team efforts.
- Provides teamwork as part of the program.
- Acknowledges that cross-functional teams are critical to success.

## Value #6 Fiscal Responsibility

"From strength to strength"

We believe a company must be financially strong in order to take advantage of opportunities and to survive problems.

Only with financial stability and soundness as a base can a company provide for its employees.

Financial strength also provides a solid bedrock on which to build an even better future.

A company can be financially strong only when all employees and management exercise fiscal responsibility.

This core value

- Expects each employee to constantly seek ways to use resources in the most effective, efficient manner possible.
- Encourages investing in support of profitable growth and good operations without putting the company at financial risk.
- Encourages the use of good, solid fiscal policies by management.

### Vaule #7 Personal Accountability

At Quill, we feel that each individual, every person at every level, is accountable for the results in areas they directly control as well as for the overall well-being of the company.

To achieve maximum results, specific responsibilities will be delegated through the entire organization. We expect each individual in the organization to accept his or her individual responsibilities—and more.

This core value encourages all individuals to hold themselves accountable for their own success as well as for the success of the entire company, going beyond their own area of responsibility, if necessary, to help achieve that success.

### Value #8 Unwavering Integrity

Integrity is the glue that holds all the rest together.

At Quill, integrity means having sound moral principles, including honesty, decency, and honor. It also means being trustworthy, caring, and dependable.

It is a character quality that allows customers, suppliers, and fellow workers to depend on us in all our dealings.

This core value expects employees to act with unwavering integrity in all that they do.

As you can see, the Quill mission statement and those values were the foundation of the culture that we lived by at Quill. We never deviated from it. Some employees found they did not like the culture and left of their own volition. People who didn't buy into our culture were let go, even if they had great ability. We felt that if they were allowed to stay, soon others would be violating some of the values and they would become meaningless. For the vast majority of the people at Quill, that mission and those values became a source of pride and a clear-cut guide on how to act and what was expected from them.

We never missed an opportunity to reinforce our values. At company events, during training sessions, at meetings, in one-on-one conversations as well as in our bonus programs and yearly profit sharing meetings—everywhere possible, we acted on and/or talked about one or more of our values.

Verbalizing your mission and values alone may work when you are a small firm where you see and talk to everyone in the company every day. But even then, it isn't the best way to create a culture. Being forced to carefully think through your mission and values by having to write them out and share them with others is a far better way to "institutionalize" those ideas so that as the company grows, every new employee knows them, and every current employee is reminded of them.

But just writing them out and giving a copy to every employee isn't enough, either. All too often the booklet ends up in a desk drawer, never to be looked at again. You must constantly communicate and reinforce the mission and values. Your actions and those of other employees are by far the strongest communicator and reenforcer. I have mentioned a few others previously but to remind you, I want to repeat them.

In addition, your entire company should abound with reminders—signs on the walls, messages on products your employees use every day, the goals set for bonuses, the way your reward system works, and, very importantly, the way in which you publicly ac-knowledge those who have done an outstanding job.

A great culture, solidly reinforced day in and day out until it becomes an integral part of everyone's minds and how everyone thinks can work wonders. It can mold the organization into an al-most invincible powerhouse that can drive you on to great success, not to mention the great pride and satisfaction it generates in everyone involved.

Not all industries are the same nor are the requirements for success within those different industries the same. And even with-in the same industry, there may be different models for success. For example, within the same industry, one company may be successful offering very low prices, another may achieve success through pro-viding extraordinary customer service, while a third does so by constantly introducing innovative products or services and a fourth by having the widest selection of products. When you think through your own mission statement, your path to success should become more obvious.

From that, decide on the critical success factors that you should focus on and build your culture accordingly. It's important to go through this exercise because it is easy to make the mistake of mix-ing critical success factors that may actually be mutually exclusive. For example, if you really want to be "the low-cost producer," it would be very dangerous to also pursue a path of being a great in-novator. Being the low-cost producer would require that you cut every single cost to the bone, while being an innovator requires putting a lot of money into research.

It is not that you can't combine some elements of various suc-cess factors. For example, being a low-cost producer while still giv-ing good customer service, can (and should) go hand in hand. But you can't be a low-cost producer while providing additional serv-ices for free.

I believe that real success requires an extreme focus on the crit-ical success factors that fit your business model. Some success factors, such as being a learning organization or being an action and results oriented organization can cut across all business models. Others are more specific to specific business models. And as the industry and competition change, there may be a need to change the business model—and then the critical success factors will also change.

At Quill, we boiled our critical success factors down to just five and we focused on them with unrelenting passion. Here they are:

1. *Provide Uncompromisingly Outstanding Customer Satisfaction* We will have a passion for constantly exceeding customer expectations, doing the ordinary things exceptionally well and constantly finding new ways to satisfy them. Through extensive research, customer feedback and analysis, we will learn our customers' needs, wants, and preferences, those they know of and those they haven't even thought of yet. We will then focus strongly on meeting and even exceeding them, providing our customers with uncompromisingly outstanding customer satisfaction that sets us apart from every other competitor.

2. *Be a Great Marketer* Using what we learn about our customers, and with the aid of a topflight marketing discipline, our goal is to market to and to satisfy each and every one of our accounts (and individuals within accounts) as they want. We will be aggressive and innovative marketers by product and by market segment.

3. *Be a Learning Organization* We must constantly learn from our customers, from the best of other companies, from each other, and from other sources. It is a mind-set we must acquire—a never ending pursuit of knowledge that is the only way to stay at the leading edge in every area of our business. It is everyone's responsibility to learn and to teach others about customers and their needs, about our company, and about effective business practices.

4. *Be a Low-Cost Producer* We will aggressively, relentlessly, and constantly drive down operating and product costs to the

lowest possible levels without compromising satisfaction, quality, ethics, or good business practices in order to provide our customers the greatest possible value.

5. *Be an Action and Results-Oriented Organization*  Success lies in the aggressive and outstanding execution of our strategies and tactics and not just in the genius of the strategies and tactics themselves. We will "go through brick walls" to achieve our goals. We will constantly strive to improve our performance in every way. But above all else, through a strong organization and excellent work force, we will act—quickly, aggressively, intelligently, ethically, and with every intention of being successful.

A good many years have passed since I wrote that Quill booklet and I am even more convinced than ever about the truths and the continuing need for what I wrote about then. It served us well at Quill, and under the continuing leadership of the team we put in place before we left, it is still serving the company well.

Just as importantly, I have had the opportunity to work with and talk with many other businesspeople and to see how lost so many of them seem to be because they don't have a clear vision of what they want to achieve. Beyond that, the news I read about the disappointing actions of so many in the business world (as well as in politics and other fields) makes the ideas in this chapter even more important and relevant.

With so many of our new business leaders graduating with MBAs from some of the most prestigious universities in the country, I begin to wonder what is being taught in those programs.

It is my absolutely firm belief that, unlike what so many so-called leaders say, it is not the stockholders, public or private, who come first. It is the customer and the employee. If you take very good care of them, and if you run the company well, then the stockholder, as a by-product of this strategy, will do very well.

In the past few years, it seems that young people fresh out of those fancy programs (and some who never went to those schools) have had the idea that they could make millions quickly and retire by the time they were in their thirties—and some did. But for most, it didn't work that way and probably never will.

I believe, more strongly than ever, that a clear vision of what you want to achieve, backed by years of experience and hard work and supported by high ethical standards, is still the surest route to success. The culture you build is also a very critical component of your success.

# Chapter 16

# Shaping a Winning Organization

"It was the best of times. It was the worst of times," Charles Dickens wrote. Often, that's how I feel about businesses, or at least the people that make up businesses. With the right people, it's the best of times; business can be fun and exciting with the burdens, ideas, and knowledge shared. With the wrong people, it's the worst of times—a true Dickensian nightmare or maybe more like something Edgar Allen Poe might have written.

Talk to people who have sold their businesses and who have retired, and one of the most common comments you will hear is how they hated the people problems and how happy they are not to have to deal with that anymore. When you talk to people who have or who want to run their own businesses after being with a large company, the reason they often give is that they can't stand the politics and all the other things that go with dealing with people in large organizations.

"People are our most important asset." That's a catchphrase used by many companies. But if they were honest, they would say *some* of our people are our most important asset. Or even more honest, "The good and talented people are our most important asset and the untalented, uncommitted people are nothing but a liability whom we would like to get rid of."

My many years in business have convinced me that one of, if not the most important tasks an entrepreneur must address is organization building. The problem is, most of us don't put the necessary focus and urgency on building, training, and motivating a really topflight organization. We always seem to be too busy solving problems, often people problems, to take the needed time. And far too often we think it costs too much to get the right people.

133

Believe me, it is not a cost. If you spend enough money and take enough time to get the right people and to give them the right training, it is an investment that pays back far more than any other way you could ever invest your time, energy, and money.

The hard part, of course, is that you have to do it while focusing on a lot of other things, such as getting business, running the company, dealing with the people you already have, and so on.

So let me give you an idea of what we learned in our 43 years of building Quill from that one man organization into an organization of more than 1,200 people. The good news is that it doesn't have to take you 43 years as it did us, because we learned six fundamental rules. Here they are.

1. Hire carefully and fire quickly.
2. Provide training so people can become the best they are capable of being.
3. Respect people, whatever their position, for the job they do.
4. Set the standards high, higher than anyone thinks they can reach, and then keep raising them.
5. Clean out the deadwood, the blockers, and the malcontents.
6. To quote President Ronald Reagan, "Trust, but verify." Put another way, give responsibility liberally but monitor carefully.

Let's go over each of these fundamental rules. Now, undoubtedly some of what I might be saying here is not relevant when you are first starting out. But it can be a guide as you grow.

So let's start with the idea of "hiring carefully and firing quickly."

Hiring carefully is an art in itself. Does the person have the skill set you need? What kind of educational background do they have? Do they have a track record, not only of competence but also of longevity at their previous jobs? Are they going to fit into your culture? Will they work hard? I've often heard it said, and I believe it, that some ability and a lot of hard work beats out more ability and a lack of hard work every time. These are only a few of the questions you need to ask yourself.

Getting the answers is not an easy task. Because of the fear of lawsuits, when you call a previous employer, often all you can get is the equivalent of name, rank, and serial number. They will not give you information about how the person performed on the job, how they got along with others, and the reason for the person leaving.

There are a few ways you can get more. One way is to ask, "Would you rehire this person?" Often you will get a yes or no answer that helps a lot, particularly if the answer is no. Or you'll hear hemming and hawing, which is the same as a no answer. Secondly, you can try to find some connection with the company the person worked for. Maybe someone in your organization knows someone in that organization, and you can try to get information that way.

You have to discount a great deal of what you read in the person's resume. Almost always when you read a resume you get the impression that the individual single-handedly grew the company or saved it amazing amounts of money. The same, by the way, is true of achievements at school. It seems as if everyone made the dean's list or some such academic high rank. Grade inflation is with us and grades mean very little these days.

You certainly must get references. People they worked for. People who worked for them. Those who were their peers. And check out all the references! You can never be too careful when hiring. I am amazed at how many companies don't check references. Of course, checking police records and credit records is critical, and it isn't all that hard to do.

You ought to also ask the prospective employee questions that would let you know what kind of person he or she is. "What do you like to do when you're not working? What are your interests?" In other words have a conversation to determine if this is a person you would like being around. Even if you don't have to be around him or her all day, your current employees do.

Finally, on hiring carefully, in some of the jobs you are hiring for, try to determine if the individual might have the credentials and capability to move up the ladder. It is worth paying a bit more to get someone who has the potential to move up to the next level and perhaps to levels beyond what you are actually hiring for. If your company will keep growing, you need a certain number of people who can take on more responsibility. If you hire well you can often get them from within your own organization when needed, and you have a much better chance of success, plus, of course, the big boost to morale when people in the company see that there is a chance for promotion.

But even with all of that, believe me, even the very best in the personnel field make mistakes when hiring. Most of the rest of us make a lot more.

Then, when we do make mistakes nearly all of us fail to face up to those mistakes and make the needed changes. We tend to live with our mistakes far too long, sometimes forever. And these mistakes keep eating away at us in the form of underperformance, spreading discontent through the organization, and just plain aggravation.

Look, the truth of the matter is that most business leaders are too soft-hearted when it comes to firing somebody. But we have to put the needs of the organization—the business you risked lots, if not everything, to build—above the feelings of an individual. Keeping a poor performer or a malcontent on is also unfair to the rest of the folks, people depending upon the success of the company for their own security and success. It also poisons the atmosphere for everyone.

When it comes to a bad promotion the same dynamic is often at work. All too often, people are promoted because they have been there for a long time. Or perhaps someone who does a really good job is promoted into a position for which they have little or no talent. It happens all the time in sales. A great salesman is promoted to be a lousy sales manager.

Or, to take one of our own experiences, when we wanted to set up an outbound telephone sales marketing group, we selected 10 of our best customer service reps and promoted them into that new department. Then, for awhile, we couldn't understand why they couldn't drive sales. Finally, we did a psychological test on those 10 folks and compared the results to the psychological test results from successful outbound telemarketers. The results showed that our best customer service reps were the type of people who enjoyed helping others. They wanted to serve people, not sell them. They were not the hard-driving, aggressive personalities needed for outbound telephone sales.

On the other hand, tests showed that the best phone sales reps were those who enjoyed the challenge of trying to sell something. They were aggressive personalities. After finding that out, we retransferred our best customer service people back into customer service where they could do what they liked to do and where they could perform well and hired more aggressive sales types for the job.

The bottom line is that to build a great organization, you must have a very good idea of the type of people and skill sets you need. Then this must guide your hiring, promoting, and, if necessary, firing.

To start with, build a good overall employment package. We wanted our pay package to be in the top quartile. We had good medical benefits and the normal vacation and holiday benefits. We had a good, but not over the top, 401(k) program. A very important part of our program, one that we played up all the time, was our very good profit sharing plan.

After just a few years in business when we had built a small organization, we introduced this plan. Personally, I hate underfunded liabilities, so a defined benefits (pension) plan was out. (And, of course, today we read in the newspapers all the horror stories about the underfunded pension plans.) With our profit sharing plan, at the end of each year, we took the profit sharing money out of the company and turned it over to a third party to administer. The company had no more control over that money after that and the plan was fully funded.

As a sidebar, in my opinion there are a number of advantages to a profit sharing plan over a defined benefits (pension) plan. First, at the end of each year, the money is put into the plan, preferably in the hands of an outside, independent firm. If the company ever went bankrupt, the employees would not lose their profit sharing money, as often happens with the usually underfunded pension plans. Next, the company does not have an underfunded liability. Finally, the employees themselves own their own profit sharing accounts and, within prudent guidelines, can decide how they want to invest the money. Finally, a profit sharing program is a powerful, free market-oriented motivator based entirely on the profitability of the company over a long period of time. A pension plan has more of the look and feel of a socialist plan and is not much of a motivator. It is looked upon by employees as a "right." When the time comes for you to choose a plan, you are far better off, for all of these reasons, to choose a profit sharing plan.

Over the years, this program became so popular and we promoted it so much within the company that it was not unusual to hear one employee tell another to get busy or to stop doing something because, "You are hurting my profit sharing." One employee who had been with us for many years and who never rose above the level of a specialist in the warehouse, retired with close to $1 million from his profit sharing fund.

Another strong part of our compensation program was our bonus plan. Bonus programs for supervisors on up helped us target people's actions toward the goals we wanted to achieve each year. But believe me, if you are going to have a bonus program, be prepared to work hard to make it a good one. You have to think long and hard about what your targets are for the year and about what each member of the bonus pool can do to help you achieve them. And you must be certain that what you are awarding is what you want people achieving, because that is what they are going to focus on, often to the exclusion of other things. You also need quarterly review sessions to measure the progress toward those goals. It's a big job, but it is worth doing if done right.

The second rule is training. Our often repeated goal at Quill was to "help everyone become the best they are capable of being so they can help Quill become the best it is capable of being."

A lot of training is on the job training and that, of course is necessary. But beyond that many companies do little or nothing, and that is a big mistake. On the job training is fine and may be all that is necessary for some "line" workers. But there is definitely a lot more needed for supervisors, managers, and other executives, including the top honcho.

Every company absolutely should have a very definite ongoing program for training supervisors. They are the folks who are in daily contact with the rest of the people. They represent the company to all the workers they supervise. No matter what you, as a leader, think or feel about sexual harassment, about racial issues, about working hard, about great customer service, or about anything else, it often is really how the supervisor feels and acts that is taken as the company's position. When a union wins an organizing drive, it is usually because of something a supervisor has been doing—or not doing.

In my opinion, as soon as you have enough people in your organization to warrant it, you should hire a first-rate labor relations law firm and have them help you shape your policies and your training program. This should include a well-thought-out, clearly written employee manual. Seek out supervisory training programs from your local business organizations as well as from your labor relations firm. Supervisors are usually folks who are promoted into that position because they have been good employees and who, hopefully, have the right qualifications. But they really know very little about being a supervisor. And, very importantly, they are making a shift from being one of the folks to being a supervisor. Their whole perspective needs to change. Supervisory training is critical.

Beyond that, whatever training is needed for managers, executives, or various specialists should be provided if your organization is going to help you succeed. For each company and each position it may be different. For example, the person in charge of personnel should belong to a local personnel management organization and attend meetings. He or she should also attend seminars and subscribe to personnel journals. And the same kind of targetted training is needed for others in your organization.

Of the third fundamental rule, "Respect people, whatever their position, for the job they do," little needs to be said. Someone has to be an awful snob not to respect every individual who deserves respect for doing a good job, regardless of the job. A custodian who keeps the place sparkling clean deserves as much respect as the vice president of marketing who comes up with a successful marketing plan. In fact, I would argue that each has a great deal to do with the success of a company. No matter how successful the marketing plan, if the work place is sloppy and unkempt, pretty soon people start doing sloppy work. And that eventually affects sales and profitability. If someone doesn't deserve respect for the kind of job they do, then they don't belong in your company.

The next rule is to "set the standards high, higher than anyone thinks they can reach, and then keep raising them." I have been criticized by any number of people, including my wife, for giving a compliment on something well done and then going on to say, "But . . . " And, of course, the criticism is right and I should learn to give a compliment and then wait a few days to come up with the "but" part of it. But that doesn't make me wrong! The "but" part is always "we could have done even better." Never be satisfied. Everything could always be done better.

I do believe that the success we had was due, in large part, to my insatiable desire to do more and to do it all better. I honestly believe that the standards should always be just beyond reach so that we have to work hard to try to reach them. And when we do reach them, after a brief period of victory, we should raise the standards even higher. I simply can't imagine ever being satisfied, for long, with having reached some goal. If you don't have goals to strive for, you begin to die. And the same is true for a business.

Our bonus programs always had minimum, target, and stretch goals, with rewards pegged to those goals. The minimum goal was something that was attainable but needed some work to achieve. The target goal really took some hard, smart work to reach. The stretch goal was pretty much out of reach. But sometimes we did reach those stretch goals. And each year, new, higher minimum, target, and stretch goals were set for each bonus participant.

The fifth rule for building a really good organization is cleaning out the "deadwoods, the blockers and the malcontents." This, in my opinion, is an important element and it is one of the most neglected. There are people in almost every organization who fit one or more of these classifications.

People who are deadwoods are those who just don't do very much of anything. They are there but they are not contributing to the overall effort. They sort of do their job, but not really. They have no drive, no ambition, no "get up and go." Someone else in their job could accomplish a great deal more.

The blockers are those who actually always seem to be against what you are trying to accomplish. They often don't agree with what you are trying to do and they almost always hate change. They keep throwing up roadblocks.

And then there are the malcontents. These are the most dangerous people to have in your organization. They are the ones who are always unhappy about almost everything. They don't like the dress policy. They don't like the benefits. They don't like a new marketing initiative. They don't like almost anything. And there's not much you can do about it because that is just the way they are. And they are not shy about sharing their opinions with anyone who will listen, which at work means their co-workers who may be perfectly happy with the way things are going. These malcontents are the types who probably prompted that old saying about how "one bad apple spoils the whole bushel."

It is critical to get rid of, first of all, the malcontents. They are dangerous. The blockers are almost as bad, and the deadwood, while not as dangerous as the other two, are just wasting money and holding back some progress. I've already talked about firing. Let me add one more thing: no excuses. Don't convince yourself,

"It's not the right time," or "What will other employees think?" or "Well, he (or she) may be miserable to be around but he (or she) knows how to do the job." Nothing but excuses. Don't let them get in the way of acting. It is always the right time to fire someone who deserves to be fired!

The final rule I have for building a good organization is, as President Reagan said, "Trust, but verify." Basically, good people want to do a good job. They take their work seriously and take pride in doing it well. And they want the company they work for to be a topflight company and to be successful.

That, in my opinion, is true from the custodian on up to the president of the company. So when you have good people, you should give them the responsibility, the authority, to do their jobs. However, and this is a very big however, it is the responsibility of every supervisor, every manager, every vice president, the president, and, if you have one, the chairman of the board, to monitor what is going on and see that everyone is doing what they should be doing and doing it well.

I have another sign in my office that says IT IS A LUXURY TO BE UNDERSTOOD. I often ask people to tell me what they think I said so I can see if they heard what I thought I had said. Believe me, when you tell people what you want done there very often is some misunderstanding. And then think about what happens when those people tell others in the organization and so on down the line of command. It's like the game Telephone, where one person whispers something into the ear of the person next to them, who then whispers it to the next person, and so on around the table. When the message finally comes back to the person who started it, it is almost always totally different from the original message.

For those two reasons—first, that people aren't perfect and second, it is rare to be immediately understood—it is critical that you always, always monitor what is happening in your organization. Well-defined reports, daily, weekly, monthly are one mechanism for doing this. Listening to what your customers are saying by reading letters of complaint and by personally taking irate customers' calls are other ways. Walking around, visiting each department, talking to folks at their workplaces is a very important way to find out what is happening.

The head of a company once said, "Everyone treats me like a mushroom, keeping me in the dark and covering me with horse manure." Don't depend on what your vice presidents or managers tell you is happening. They all have a vested interest in making things look good. You must talk with the order packer, the customer service rep, and so on. You must even, sometimes, look into piles of paper on someone's desk to see if things are being handled in a timely manner. And most of all, you should hold people responsible for the results.

Now, you've got the five rules for building an organization. The last step is choosing a structure. There seem to be two extremes in organizations. The first is where far too many people have titles. The place is loaded with vice presidents and so on. Too many titles usually is a negative. From what I have observed, once someone gets a title, certain work is, in their opinion, below them. Also, pay scales are usually tied in with titles, and when titles are given out easily, people often are being paid far more than they are worth. It often amused me, after we sold to Staples, to see how many very, very young people were vice presidents. The only requirement seemed to be that they had graduated from an Ivy League school with an MBA; whether they actually knew anything or could run anything seemed not to matter.

It was funny, and costly, when one of these young vice presidents began telling my brother Harvey who had years of experience in designing and building our very good systems and warehouses how a new warehouse should be laid out, according to the consultant she used. Harvey explained how her plan was far too complicated and relied far too heavily on conveyor belt after conveyor belt. But the warehouse got built her way. All of Harvey's observations proved to be correct. It was a costly mistake.

Now, I don't want to knock Staples too much because they did have a lot of good, experienced people in the organization and they worked harder than most any other company I have seen. They just passed out too many titles too easily.

On the other extreme is a "flat" organization, where there are very few titles. Frankly, I favor the flat organization, but for a long time we carried that too far. Because my brothers and I formed such a strong team, each covering a different area of the business, we felt we didn't need vice presidents at all. We basically had ourselves and then managers for each of the departments. All the managers reported to one of us. We strongly resisted giving out titles.

But pressures began to build. We weren't getting any younger. Competition was increasing. We were getting bigger. There was a lot more to do. There were a lot of ideas on how to grow the business even faster, but we were just too busy to implement many of them.

So we began to look for people with the skill levels we needed to come in and take on some of the leadership roles. We soon learned that we couldn't convince this type of person to come with us unless we made them a vice president and gave them the money and, just as importantly, the responsibilities and authority to go along with the title. For a company that prided itself on its very flat organization, giving out those titles was a big step. (The money part was not a problem.)

Although we didn't realize it at the time, hiring someone at the vice presidential level signaled a significant change in the power structure of the company. The first vice president we hired was the vice president of merchandising. Our previous manager of merchandising had quit and I had stepped in to handle that job, along with everything else I was doing, until we could find someone. It took about eight months (eight very tough months for me) until we found someone who had the exact experience we needed and was at the level we needed.

Soon after that, we hired a vice president of operations, who reported to my brother Harvey (and when we sold, became president of the company—and a very good president) and a few years later we hired a vice president of human resources, who reported to my brother Arnold. All three came from much larger firms and had been accustomed to having a good deal of authority. While we were slow in giving up authority, they were fast at grabbing it.

Soon, these vice presidents were training younger individuals beneath them, giving them more and more responsibility. And it wasn't long before these individuals started getting job offers. See, our company had built a reputation as a good place to work, and a real hotbed of talent, so headhunters were trying to raid Quill. Our response? We created a new level, that of director, reporting to the vice presidents, and gave these individuals 40 percent to 50 percent raises and a larger bonus potential. That was some of the best money we ever spent. In fact, building this whole management team was one of the best investments we had ever made. We were foolish for not having done it sooner. But still, getting a title at Quill was something that had to be earned and was not given easily.

And while I have made some remarks about Ivy League MBA types, we did believe in the importance of what can be learned in an MBA program. We made sure all our young executives, after they had been with us for a number of years and had a lot of experience, enrolled in a local evening and weekend MBA program. To me, an MBA degree without a lot of experience is just another piece of paper. Leveraged with experience it can add power to an individual's efforts.

In any event, the proof of how well we had built the organization is that now, nine years after we sold the company, that same team is in place, with one of them becoming president, running and building Quill to even greater heights.

It took us a very long time to figure all this out, but perhaps what we learned will help you get there a lot faster.

# Chapter 17

# Who Controls Your Life?

We've all felt it: life seems to be spinning out of control. There's too much to do and not enough time to do it all. The desk is piled high with paperwork. There are too many unfinished and partly finished tasks, all weighing heavily on your mind. There's no time to quietly tackle the tasks at hand and finish them. And no time to just sit and think, or to read or relax.

As long as you are active, all of this applies to your business life and to your personal life. I thought that when we sold the business, I would finally be able to get everything under control. But then I became so active in various other endeavors that I often found myself back in the same old condition.

Finally, I had to think very hard about how I could get control of my life. No longer involved in the day-to-day running of a business helped give me a better perspective on what I should have done while running it, as well as what I should be doing now in my personal life, which includes investing, philanthropy, and being involved with two businesses, not to mention golf and a few other things.

In the first place, it's all about time and tasks and how you match them up: how you allocate time and what tasks you really should do and what you should have someone else do, if they need to be done at all. That sounds simple, I know. Unfortunately in practice, it rarely is.

I have found that a good beginning is to make two lists. The first list is of those things you, personally, must do and those you want to do. The second list includes those things that you are doing that you really, truthfully, don't need to be doing and those things that you, yourself, don't need to do, things that others can do as well, or even better.

In that second list there may be some things that are also on your first list. There are things that you want to do, but you just don't get around to finishing them and they keep nagging at you. For example, writing this book. I've wanted to do it for the past 18 years (according to the date on my first notes), and I finally started it about a year ago. I'm on the last few chapters, but things keep interfering with my finishing. So to satisfy my "want to/must do" and my "don't want to/don't need to do" lists, I am carving out some major chunks of time to get the book done. There are a few other such items on my lists, items that will just require the discipline to get them done and off both lists.

To start getting control of your life, as an entrepreneur and the head of a business, you must recognize that there are certain things that you really are responsible for and that few, if any others, can do. Those things, and believe me, there are very few of them, are what you really get paid for and that must be on your "need to do" list. Then, there are other things in the business that you want to be involved with because you enjoy them. They, too, go on the first list. But with these you should be selective because if you spend too much time on them, they prevent you from doing those "need to do" tasks.

Then make out a list of those things you don't want to do. Some of these can be things that really, if you think hard about them, really don't need to be done. Others are things that do need to be done but that can be done by someone else. This last category is one that is tough for most ego-driven entrepreneurs to deal with because they feel that only they can do certain things. But if you build your organization with good people, there are others who can do many of the things that you are doing. And the truth of the matter is that they can often do them better than you can if, for no other reason, they can spend more time on them. And, although it is hard to admit, they might even be better at that particular job than you are.

Here I would like to comment about hiring a good administrative assistant. The mistake that I see businesspeople making time and again is not paying enough to get someone who is really outstanding, someone who can help relieve them of the load. I think that you have to ask yourself just exactly whose time you are paying for. For example, when it comes to an administrative assistant, it's really *your* time that you are paying for, not his or her time. A really good administrative assistant can take over a lot of what you are doing. It's worth paying for and getting the best. And after you pay for it, make sure you are getting what you paid for or keep making changes until you do. It's the quality of your life that's involved.

In any event, after you complete your lists, go over them very carefully. Take an especially aggressive look at your "want to/must do" list. Keep going over it, constantly asking if *you* are the one who must do some of the things on the list. Go over it with someone else: your partner, your assistant, your spouse. Keep asking, Can someone else do some or all of any of the listed items? At the very least, maybe someone else can do a lot of the "grunt" work on an item and you just make the final decisions. Pare that list down to the essentials, those things that *only* you can and must really do plus a few of the things you really enjoy doing.

Also, carefully go over the "don't want to/don't need to do" list and make decisions on those things that simply don't need doing at all or don't need doing by you, and decide to either eliminate them or decide who should handle them.

As part of this whole endeavor, learn to be very careful about undertaking any new endeavors. One of the most powerful words in controlling your life is the word, "no." Believe me, it is a real art and a difficult one to learn to say no at the proper time. You are constantly besieged on all fronts for pieces of your time. You have to learn when it is in your and your company's best interest to invest some of your time listening to someone or doing something. But at the same time, you need to learn when it isn't worth the investment of your time. And believe me, this gets very difficult when friends or business acquaintances are asking. It's hard enough when strangers ask.

On top of all that, there is the matter of ego. How many of us can resist when some organization wants to "honor" us? But on the other hand, while that honor usually involves giving money, it also involves a lot of time from you or a member of your staff. For a cause you really believe in, it's worth doing. But many times it isn't. And there are many other time-consuming things that your ego gets involved with. You really must control what your ego wants to lead you into.

The other way to keep control of your own life, I talk about in Chapters 18 and 19—get control over reports and meetings.

Besides making the lists and cutting way back on meetings and reports, here's the magic—well, not really magic—to getting control over your own life. Remember, your job is simple: it's to make your company successful. It's not to be spent frittering away your time on things that really aren't critical to that mission or on things that really can be done just as well by others.

- *Most of us don't prioritize well, if at all.* Not all the things we have to do are equal. Some get better, more important results than others. Those are the ones that should get the highest priority. We can't do everything so we should either drop or assign to others the lower-priority jobs.

- *Most of us don't aggressively delegate jobs to others.* What conceited asses we are, thinking that we have to do everything. Whoever came up with the line, "If you want something done right, you should do it yourself," was an idiot. Too often too many entrepreneurs believe that. And it is amazing how often people at the top don't take the time to train someone else to do the job and then they, themselves spend multiples of that time doing the jobs themselves.

- *Most of us don't spend enough time thinking about whether the job should be done at all.* And if it is decided that the job does need to be done, enough time isn't spent thinking about the best, most efficient way to do it. Too often we just plow ahead, spending whatever time it takes to get the job done—the old way.

So who really does control your life? If you are smart, you will make damned sure that it is you. If you are going to live to be eighty, there are only 960 months in your life. By the time you are out of school, 264 or so of those months are gone. If you want to retire by the time you are sixty-five, then there are only 516 months in your working life during which you can really build something. Cut that by the time during each day that you are not working, by weekends, by vacations, and by sickness, and you are probably down to about 135 months.

That isn't a lot of time to build a great business, unless you take control of your life.

# Chapter 18

# Easing the Burden

I've spent a lot of time in this book talking about how hard you have to work and how you can't be intimidated by that prospect. But now, let me put that into its proper perspective. Digging ditches is hard work. Finding a cure for cancer can be hard work. Unfortunately, too many of us who are the leaders of our companies spend too much of our time doing the equivalent, figuratively, of digging ditches and believing that we are working hard. We're not—at least not working hard at what we should be doing.

I often used to say that I got paid for about 10 percent of my time. What I did with the other 90 percent, others could have done as well or even better. And the shame of this situation is that I was not doing as good a job as I could have on what I was spending just 10 percent of my time on.

As president of the company, it was my responsibility, my job, to lead the company, to make sure we were building the right kind of organization, that we were doing everything possible to grow the company and to make it more profitable. Along with my brothers, our job was to be making sure that we were servicing our customers as we promised and that all parts of the company were meshing well to achieve our goals. Our job was to motivate others to help us achieve all our goals. All of these things should have taken the vast majority of our time. Instead, we spent most of our time bogged down in details—"digging ditches"—tasks that others could and should have been doing.

I told you about that sign on my desk, the one that read JACK MILL-ER WILL DO ONLY THOSE THINGS THAT ONLY JACK MILLER CAN DO. Unfortunately, I didn't pay enough attention to that sign. And my assistant didn't force me to live up to what it said. Interestingly, throughout most of my "retirement" I had the same assistant (She has since passed away). We both had matured and had learned a lot, and we both worked hard to live up to the message in that sign. In fact, she kept asking me, "What are you doing that I can do for you?"

It's amazing how many things she had taken from me that I was just doing out of habit. It freed me up to be involved with many different, new interests. And it's just because we were both paying attention to that sign. But, when I was president of Quill, I kept doing too many of those things that others could have been doing just as well or better. And, looking back, I think that had two major consequences.

First, although we grew well, 15 percent or so a year, we didn't grow as fast as we could have if I had, instead, focused all my energies and time where I should have.

Second, as part of that, I was always very busy, too busy to take many vacations, so busy I "had to" work Saturdays and take work home for evenings and Sundays. In the early years, much of that may have been needed because we couldn't afford much of an organization and my brothers and I had to wear a lot of hats. But, as time went on, it became a habit, a hard habit to break. Frankly, I was being overpaid for most of the work I was doing.

Let me give you an example. In the early days, I did the layouts and wrote all the copy for our mailing pieces. Believe me, that took many an evening and most weekends. As time went on, we built an advertising department. But for a very long time, I still proofread every bit of copy. After I finally stopped doing that, I still insisted that we have a meeting to discuss each mailing piece and to give me a chance to comment on the overall look of the piece, the headlines, the product presentations, and so on.

So the first rule in this chapter is to take a hard look at what you are spending your time on. Some consultants suggest you keep a log of what you do during each day so you get a better idea of where your time is spent. Maybe, though my guess is with a little reflection you know what you are doing with your time.

Then, prioritize. Most of us think that we get paid for working hard. But what we really get paid for is results, and that means working hard at the right things. In every company of every size, resources of time and people and money are in scarce supply. At every level, in every job, and particularly at the highest level, effort must be focused on those things that will yield the highest results. As a leader, make sure that you are focusing on those things that are of the highest priority for you and your company. The other things that are not a high priority for you should be made a high priority for others in the organization.

After you have prioritized, be very aggressive in delegating jobs to others further down the chain. Too often, people feel they are the only ones who can do things right, and too often, they don't feel they have the time to train someone else to do the job. Yet they seem to have the time to spend doing the job that someone else could be doing. There's a lot of mixed up thinking going on. You *must* delegate every job you can, and you *must* be aggressive about it.

Then, and this is a very big potential time saver, most of us don't really, seriously think about whether certain work should be done at all. There's a lot of stuff going on in every company that simply doesn't have to be done. It's a waste of time—for anyone to be doing. So look at every job being done and ask others to do the same with an eye toward eliminating the job. Or, with an eye toward streamlining it or the procedure. An awful lot of time is wasted throughout the organization doing things in a certain, in-efficient way just "because this is the way we have always done it."

And that brings me to two of the biggest time wasters that every executive faces almost every day: (1) the overabundance of reports and information much of which he or she doesn't need and most of which are too long and too wordy and (2) meetings that consume a great deal of time and often lead to little action. To be productive, to streamline your organization and, just as important, ease your burden, you have to attack both of these.

Cut the waste out of reports. Just imagine for a moment how much productivity in the United States is wasted by people reading reports that they, in their position, don't need to read. Or reading reports that are too lengthy and could be cut by 50 percent or more. Give me a nickel for every wasted minute and I could have funded my retirement quickly.

Here's a list of four ways to cut down on report waste.

1. Have someone look at every report being generated in your company to determine whether it needs to be generated, whether people are reading and acting upon it, whether every recipient needs every portion of the report.
2. Eliminate reports that are not needed or used.
3. Make sure the reports are going to only those who really need them and even then, that they get only the part of the report that they need.
4. Make sure that reports are used. If you are going to spend money preparing and distributing reports, they should become instruments of action. If they aren't read, understood, and acted upon, then they are truly a total waste of time, money, and effort.

With the advent of computers, this problem has become even worse because it's too easy to send reports, all reports, to a list of names.

Cut down on meetings. They are the scourge of the modern organization. There simply are too many meetings, most lasting too long and most with too many attendees.

Of course, some meetings are necessary, even helpful. But even the good ones usually have too many people. Rule number one about meetings should be that people may attend ONLY if they can really add something or really have a need to know.

More often than not, though, meetings are a waste of time, held for no good reason. Some are held just because people are afraid of making a decision themselves and want to be able to spread the blame if something goes wrong. Or perhaps there are meetings that keep being scheduled long after the need for them has disappeared just because they have been going on.

Research done by an outfit called MCI World Com Conferencing indicates that "busy professionals are now spending nearly three hours every day in meetings and more than a third of those polled said the meetings are unproductive." How can you keep meetings from slowing productivity at your business? There are six things I have found that help.

1. Don't have a meeting unless absolutely essential. A phone call, a chat at lunch, stopping by someone's office, or some other informal method often can accomplish the purpose.

2. If a meeting is absolutely necessary, include only those who absolutely must be there. For each meeting carefully decide who has a real need to be there. And each invitee should question whether he or she really must attend the meeting, and if they decide that the meeting would be a waste of their time, they should be empowered to decide not to attend.

3. Keep meetings short. There is no magic in one hour or any other particular time frame. In fact, when a time frame is set, whoever sets it should err on the side of less time rather than more. End the meeting when the task is finished, not when the clock says it's time, with earlier being better than later.

4. Have an agenda and stick with it. If you can't run a tight meeting, find somebody who can. Somebody has to be the boss of every meeting.

5. Someone should be designated to take notes at each meeting and should publish these notes for each participant. These notes should be the basis for actions to be taken and for a follow-up system to see that the actions are taken.

6. Meetings should start on time, even if some of the attendees aren't there yet. There is no excuse for keeping six or 10 people sitting around wasting time because someone didn't have the courtesy to be on time.

Without a doubt, it takes a lot of hard work to build a successful company. Unfortunately, sometimes people work very hard and still can't seem to achieve the success they are seeking. Of course, it may be that the product or service they are offering isn't what the consumer wants. Or perhaps they simply don't have the ability needed. But it could very well be that they are working very hard digging ditches and not focusing on those things that will bring them that sought-after success. In many cases, this is the problem.

Of course, once you stop digging those ditches and begin to focus on what you really should be focusing on you potentially face the problem of coming into the office and sitting down at an empty desk and saying to yourself, "Now what can I do to make this company more successful?" Believe me, it is a lot easier to sit down at that desk and have a pile of paper on one side that you can dig into, so that at the end of the day you can say, "Well, I finished going through all those reports and reading all the memos, so I did something today."

But then, that really isn't what you are getting paid for, is it?

George Halas, the legendary football coach, once said, "A football game requires 3.5 hours of elapsed time, 1.0 hours of clock time, and 5.3 minutes of actual playing time." Don't let your business life be a football game.

Seneca the Younger (4 B.C. to A.D. 65) once said, "It's not that we have too little time; it's too much time we do not use to the fullest."

Okay, no more time spent on this subject!

# Chapter 19

# Doing More by Doing Less

The topic in the last chapter, Easing the Burden, is so important that I would like to expand on it.

I always used to wonder how someone could be the head of Sears Roebuck or General Motors and handle it all when it was taking me 50 to 60 hours just to run Quill. As I have already said, the answer, it seems to me, is that it all has to do with really doing only those things that you, as a result of your position, and perhaps ability, can and should do and then letting others take on the rest of it. The truth of the matter is that there are many things that take a tremendous amount of time to do that others can do, freeing you up to focus on some very important issues.

Most businesses don't achieve the success that they should because the leaders of these businesses are so busy becoming personally involved with everyday issues that others can handle (probably just as well or better) that they just don't have the time or energy to focus on the strategic issues. In fact, they are so busy and so tuckered out that they don't even want to grow the business because it would just be more work for them, when they feel they are already overburdened.

This is such a common phenomena that I'm surprised there aren't more books, articles, and seminars on it.

I was guilty of the same thing. What a waste of my time and energy! How much bigger we could have been if I had focused on some other issues that could have led us on to even greater success.

So how does this happen, even when we sort of realize that it is happening, and why don't we do something about it? I've come to the conclusion that for most of us, it happens because we start out as workers. When we start our businesses, we have to pitch in just about everywhere. We learn a lot about many areas of the operation. And as we grow and we hire people, we usually tend to hire just at the level to do a particular job. So we always feel that we have to be involved to make sure the job is done well. We should hire the best people we can for each particular job, then, after they prove themselves, we should let go. What I have found is that when good people were focusing on a particular area of the business, they soon knew more than I did and could do the job better than I could.

It's hard to do because there is more at work here, and that is that we all like to do the familiar. Doing what we know how to do is very comforting. Venturing out into new territory is daunting for almost everyone. Yet, if you are going to grow as an executive and you are going to lead your company toward greater success, that is exactly what you must do. Instead of focusing on the exact words used in the headlines in our advertising pieces, I should have spent more time focusing on the better use of our assets and abilities.

Working with the familiar is only one reason why executives tend to spend so much time on things that others can do. As I said in the last chapter, another reason is the comfort of coming in with a desk full of paperwork to do and then, by the end of the day, having all or most of it done. Gosh, you were busy all day and you actually got something done.

On the other hand, just think of what it would be like to go into your office in the morning with an absolutely clean desk, no paperwork to do, no phone calls to make. Your job is to take a blank sheet of paper and to create, actually create, some new concept or plan. *That* is a daunting, even frightening task.

Obviously, none of us can really get to that position. There are always things going on, situations that need to be handled, calls that need to be made, and so on. But getting as close as possible to that position is a goal every leader should be striving for. And let me tell you, some ways of getting there are pretty fundamental. Let me give you one, personal, example.

As I said in the previous chapter, I had a good assistant at Quill, but when we sold, she left to work for a much larger organization. When my brother Harvey and I set up a family office, I hired another assistant. As we got involved with real estate, with philanthropy, and then another business I bought, the paperwork and phone calls began to pile up. Writing this book was getting delayed. Frankly, I was getting frustrated. A lot of things weren't getting done. My files were sort of a mess. I was good at filing, or at least at putting papers into folders, but very poor at finding items I needed.

Finally, my assistant and I agreed that she should leave. Fortunately for me, the executive at the larger company that my old assistant was working for retired, so she and I reconnected and she came back to work for me. Within a few months, everything was up-to-date. My files were all straightened out.

Just imagine that happening throughout the organization. On the other hand, imagine it not happening and imagine what can and actually does happen when the leader doesn't focus on the main issues but stays involved with the 90 percent of things that others could be handling.

Imagine a huge water pipe, maybe five feet in diameter. Just think of how much water, under full pressure, could rush through such a pipe. Can you just see the flood of water coursing through that pipe? But now think of that huge pipe as being squeezed down at the end to just a one-inch opening. Can you picture how that torrent of water becomes just a relatively small jet of water and that whole big potential back in the five-foot diameter area virtually comes to a halt?

With that image in mind, think about a business with lots of eager, capable people—ready, willing, and able to handle the work and even to come up with ideas on how to make things happen even better. And then think of a manager, a vice president, or president who insists on having to be involved with and who needs to approve every single thing. Managers, obviously, should be involved with and must approve a lot more than the vice presidents, who should be involved with and who must approve a lot more than the president.

But just carry on the thought of that leader who must micromanage just about everything. You can envision that potentially massive flow of ideas and effort almost coming to a halt. You can also easily envision a leader who takes home a briefcase full of work, works long hours including weekends, seldom takes a real vacation, and most importantly never has enough time to really give much thought to long-term, more strategic initiatives. Then you can also visualize a company where changes come slowly, where people feel frustrated, and where they often lose their enthusiasm, with the really good ones sometimes leaving.

This sort of blockage of creativity and entrepreneurial spirit doesn't just happen in big companies. It can happen to the smallest. My dad was a great salesman. But he spent virtually all of his time in the live poultry store waiting on women who wanted a chicken or a duck. When I was in the food business, I ran across someone who made chicken pot pies and who bought 5,000 pounds or so of chicken meat at a time. I introduced him to my dad and soon Dad was supplying him. There were one or two other accounts like that that Dad serviced. He could have built upon these accounts. He could have gotten much bigger using his great selling ability instead of spending 10 hours a day in the store waiting on customers. When I questioned him, he said, "I can't leave Abe (his brother) here to handle all the business by himself." But he really could have hired a capable person to do that and then focused his attention and abilities where he could have built a much bigger, much more profitable wholesale operation. He had the talent. But he let it get blocked.

When they were finally forced to close the store because they couldn't compete with the chain stores, Dad set up a desk in our office and spent his time building up the wholesale business. Toward the end, he had a nice little business going and was working about half a day every day. If he had done that when he was younger, he could have built quite a business. But he was spending all his time selling one chicken at a time to ladies who walked into the store. He spent very little time on the few wholesale accounts he had and no time in expanding that potentially very much larger part of the business.

In a microcosm, that is exactly what is going on to a lesser or larger degree, in most businesses. To be a successful entrepreneur, you have to know where to focus your time and talent.

Recently, someone in a family business asked me, "How do you know when you are micromanaging?" In other words, he was asking me how much managing and oversight you should have on what is going on and how much is too much. This is a critical question because I am not advocating that you just turn things over to others and walk away. You are, after all, the person who is responsible for the success or failure of the company. And, ultimately, there is no way you can say, when something goes wrong, "That wasn't my job."

One key to being able to let go, of course, is hiring well. The other is setting up systems that let you know exactly how the business is operating at any given moment. It is important to set up daily, weekly, monthly reports that give you a bird's eye view of what is going on, reports that are carefully reviewed either by you alone or with a small group of others. A line by line review of the monthly financial statement is one such report. But every business can develop reports that will highlight the critical numbers and events for that business. And the minute something seems out of line, you have to look into it. You can't just shrug it off.

Then there's the concept of "managing by walking around." Personally I don't think there is anything that can replace this for getting the pulse of the business and for surfacing any problems. And I don't mean just walking around to be seen or to just talk with the managers. I mean walking around into different areas of the company, without the manager, and talking to the person who talks to customers on the phone or talking to the shipping clerk, and so on. It's amazing what you see and learn. Dirty warehouse floors and sloppy work areas never show up in reports but they can alert you to poor management and potential problems. A pile of unanswered correspondence in customer service is also something that doesn't show up on reports but is a sign of a major problem.

My point is that letting go of the tasks you don't need to be doing doesn't mean you are letting go of the important operations of your company. See, there are ways that you can let go of many of the time-consuming jobs that you used to be involved with every day and still keep pretty close control of what is going on. In fact, you can probably get an even better idea by getting out from under the day to day tasks you don't need to be doing.

So how did I answer the question? I said that you know that you are micromanaging when you insist on being involved with every decision, when you insist on having control of everything that is going on. You have to let people do their jobs. You must have systems in place so you get early warning signals when something isn't going as it should.

Your constant, ongoing job as a leader is to always look for ways you can be "doing more by doing less." Frankly, even if somebody may not do some job quite as well as you might, you usually ought to let someone else do the job so you can focus on the really critical issues.

# Chapter 20

# Your Growth as a Leader

You know that a business is going to stop growing when you hear the head of it saying something like, "I'm burned out," or "How many pairs of pants can you wear at one time?" or "There are just so many balls I can juggle," or "How many meals can you eat?" or some such comment. It's really a sign that they have never made the jump from being an entrepreneur who has to control everything that's going on to becoming a business leader who can delegate and manage.

For example, the uncle I worked for had a very nice $5 million plus business. For five years after college, I worked there as a traveling salesman. The company was exceptionally well run from the viewpoint of giving great customer service, controlling costs, and being very competitively priced. I learned a lot about how to run a company from him. But I also learned, by watching my uncle, a good bit about how not to work as a CEO.

My uncle, who was a really great guy, usually got to the office around 9:00 A.M., had coffee, and read the morning paper. Then a good part of the day, before he left at around 5:00 P.M., he would spend at his desk, mostly going through paperwork, reviewing figures, and so on. He spent some time walking around the plant, talking with people. He never worked on Saturdays.

I don't once remember him ever having any kind of strategic planning meeting. Even after I took over the advertising for the company—a task he had previously handled himself—there were no meetings about what to do, where we were going, how we were going to get there. Everything seemed to be done on a case by case, account by account basis. Not that he didn't have a good, basic overall

165

strategy. It was just that there never seemed to be a relentless push to do more, to go beyond the tried and true. Yes, he always pushed to get more accounts, but only by taking the same old approaches.

My uncle had built a good business and led a comfortable life. But he never grew in his position as a true leader. And there is nothing wrong with what he did and how he did it, as long as you are not trying to build a large company. What he did, he did well. His customer service was outstanding. His attention to detail was great. But he spent too much time getting tied down by the minutia of the business.

The dictionary defines a "plateau" as "a relatively level area that is at a higher elevation than the land around it." Or "(a) a level state of development; (b) a period of little progress following a period of rapid progress."

In business, it can be defined as a time to catch your breath or a time of winding down. Either way, it represents a loss of momentum. It is not to be enjoyed but, rather, to be recognized as the danger sign that it is.

Most critically, allowing your company to slow down destroys the aggressive motivation that should run through a business. Many employees, usually the best ones, see their career growth threatened and begin to think of leaving for better opportunities. The mediocre ones hang onto their jobs. It becomes difficult to attract good talent. If the period of no growth continues for some time, the organization becomes one that then perpetuates a no-growth culture because the mediocre employees now dominating the culture know no other way.

Suppliers begin to view the company as an "also ran," a company that isn't going to be able to help them achieve their own growth goals and therefore a company not being given their best deals. Customers eventually pick up on what is happening when they begin to notice a lack of new products or innovative new services that are being offered by competition. At some time, even if business volume doesn't decrease, competitors have passed you by.

The main reason that smaller, privately owned companies plateau is because they have grown as large as their owners' talents and abilities can take them and still have complete, hands-on control. Even if these CEOs want their companies to get larger, they simply don't know how, or are unwilling to learn how or to take the next step, to give up some control, to bring in more talented people, and to give them real responsibility. They constantly bemoan the fact that they have too much to do, that they have to do everything. And they invent rationalizations explaining away their lack of real leadership. (If you ever find yourself invoking any of these, heed the warning signs and make a change—in yourself.)

- *"It's a custom business."* That is, everything requires a special decision by the business owner. Customer contact, designs, pricing—nothing has been standardized so that others can handle the jobs. The business owner is convinced that only he or she is capable enough of handling what needs to be done.
- *"Face it, I can only trust myself—completely."* "I have to be involved with everything." "The help is going to steal from me." "They're not going to work unless I am there every minute." "They're going to make dumb mistakes that will cost me a lot of money." On and on that kind of thinking goes. It all adds up to getting, well, not very far.
- *The disappearance of wrinkles in the belly.* The threat of starvation is one hell of a motivator. The desire for the good things of life is not quite as good a motivator—but it is a fairly good second. But sooner or later there comes a time when most entrepreneurs look around and begin to think, "I've got my Mercedes. I belong to a good country club. I've got some security and my family is taken care of. I owe it to myself to enjoy life a little. After all how many pairs of pants can I wear? How many meals can I eat?"

- *"I'm not getting any younger."* At some point, entrepreneurs, like everyone else, begin to realize that there aren't that many years left. But what they do with that realization is what makes all the difference. If they don't have a son, daughter, or ready heir to the business they feel they can trust to take over, they either sell out if they can, or they stop trying to grow the business in what they perceive (usually misguidedly) as an effort to preserve the wealth they have built. In addition to being dangerous, this can also be very frustrating to the next generation, often causing them to leave the business, which puts more of the burden back onto the aging entrepreneur.

- *"It's just no more fun. I'm burned out."* How I hate that phrase "burned out." To hear a sixty-year-old who has worked hard all his or her life say it is bad enough. But to hear a much younger entrepreneur say it is tragic. In my opinion, most people who say they are burned out were never really ignited in the first place. But for too many entrepreneurs there comes a time when running the business has become repetitive, the same old problems have to be resolved, the competition is tougher (or seems to be), it's not the same industry, the old camaraderie is gone, and so on.

Once when I was at a funeral, the wife of a very good friend, who had passed away some years before, said to me, "You and Howard (her late husband) were very lucky because your companies kept growing and you constantly were changing jobs." She was right on target because that is exactly what happens when your company grows and you grow with it. So how do you make sure your business keeps growing and that you keep growing with it, and as a result your job keeps changing?

First of all, remember that old saying, "Fish and businesses begin to decay from the head down."

So in order not to begin to decay, I believe that there are several ingredients that must be present and several steps that must be taken. The first, and perhaps most important, ingredient is an insatiable desire for growth—an enjoyment of the "game," a desire to stretch yourself to your limits, limits that far exceed any needs satisfied by normal success. I was never a star athlete nor a great musician or painter. But I could and did shine in my area of the business world. I satisfied that desire in me to "shine" through my business. And it has given me far greater pleasure than I could possibly express. It wasn't just about making money. That was sort of a by-product of running and growing a good company.

Second is the desire and willingness to build a good organization, a lean and hungry organization with the same burning desire for growth (and for running a good company). Building a good organization is absolutely essential to building a good company. Even the strongest, most powerful, smartest CEO can take a company only so far by themselves. And that, frankly, isn't very far. That same type of individual, backed by a really good organization, can take a company as far as they want to go.

But there is also something more that is needed. And that is the continued growth and development of the entrepreneur, of you. That is what I was referring to earlier when I talked about what my friend said about her late husband and me. We were constantly "changing jobs," throughout our entire careers. From day one in my one man business, I was the president, the CEO and the chairman of the board. Forty-three years later, when we sold our 1,400 plus person business, I was still the president, the CEO, and the chairman of the board. But I was a very different person and the jobs I was doing were very different.

I started out on the street selling, picking up merchandise from the wholesaler, rushing back to Dad's chicken store to wrap the customer orders and then rushing to get them to the United Parcel depot before 6:00 P.M. so they could be delivered the next day. Forty-three years later, I was doing none of those jobs. I was deeply involved with strategic planning, reinforcing our mission statement and values throughout our nationwide organization, financial planning, estate planning, and much, much more. Even merchandising and marketing, which were my main loves, were areas where I was only lightly involved, with just general oversight.

I spent a good chunk of those 43 years educating myself. A lot of the education came from constantly questioning what I was doing running the business. A lot of it also came from reading about business in general and about my own industry in particular and from attending conventions and seminars in both the office products industry and the direct marketing field. And, just as importantly, I got a great education talking with others in office products and in direct marketing and who run other types of businesses.

Constantly educating yourself, and having but one goal you are striving for—growing and building the business—makes sure you never get bored, never burn out, and never get stuck on a business plateau. Business remains fun and, as you progress, it becomes even more fun.

Ability and talent are important. But I will take a man or woman with lesser talent and stronger drive over someone with great talent and little drive. "Drive" defines success in an entrepreneur. There will be moments when you look at what you have achieved and feel a sense of accomplishment. But more often, no matter how successful your endeavor, you will be looking at success with a critical eye, seeing shortcomings, feeling frustrated, perhaps, that you are not doing more. Does that sound terrible? Not in my mind, because never being satisfied is what drives performance. Being satisfied, well, that will drive your business to the plateau and nowhere further.

The natural outgrowth of never being satisfied is being a critic, a constant judge of others as well as of yourself. Frankly, it isn't always a comfortable position. Not all entrepreneurs are willing or even constitutionally able to take on such an aggressive leadership position. But if you are going to head up the company and if you want to be successful, then you are the only one who can do it, or make sure it gets done. The degree to which you do so will go a long way toward determining the quality of your company and the degree of your success.

None of this comes easily. It's a constant, evolving growth that you as a leader must go through if you expect your company to be also constantly evolving and growing. Some people by nature can't do it. Others take to it quite naturally. And a great many more have to really work at it. But I know that it can be done and that it all starts with the vision, the desire, and the drive to become successful.

Even with all of this, with the constant desire to be even more successful and with never really being satisfied, I can tell you that the journey is one of the most enjoyable experiences you can have and once you retire, it is something that you constantly get pleasure from as you look back at it. Succeeding is great.

## Chapter 21

# Someone Changed the Rules.
# Why Wasn't It Me?

In addition to my suburban, or "country" (as my wife likes to call it) home, I have a condo in downtown Chicago, on the fifty-seventh floor of our building. One of the views is looking west over almost the entire city. In the foreground, just a mile or two from the condo, I get a magnificent view of the former headquarters of Montgomery Ward with its 20- or 30-story-tall office building and its several block long, multistory warehouse along the Chicago river. The problem is, it is no longer Montgomery Ward's. Their headquarters office building is now a high-rise residential condo and the monumental warehouse has been converted to lower-cost, low-rise residential condominiums.

Ward's is no longer. They closed their doors in 2001, a victim of changes and innovations in the marketplace that they did not bring about themselves and were, for some reason, unable to adapt to.

The ironic part of this is that Ward's was established, in 1872 by Aaron Montgomery Ward, as an innovative method of "retailing." According to company history, Ward founded his company as a mail order operation because he was "concerned by the high prices rural Americans were paying for shoddy goods." His solution was to deliver quality products at reasonable prices to consumers in their homes.

Sears, of course, soon followed the same path. Both of them later opened retail outlets and both grew to be giants in retailing.

Today, Ward's is totally out of business and Sears dropped their major mail order catalog and is a second-tier competitor in retailing, far behind Wal-Mart, a relative newcomer, and other big-box retailers. The rules had changed and neither of these two giants were the ones who changed them.

The lesson of this chapter is that the rules are always changing and that if you want to stay in the game you must be the rule changer, or at least a fast adapter. You can't afford to become ossified in your historical way of doing things, which may not meet the new market challenges. It happened in my industry. Unfortunately, too many companies are not able to make the change.

The story in the office products industry is very similar to the story of Ward's, Sears, and Wal-Mart. In 1986 Tom Stemberg was looking for a job and he needed some office supplies. He went to his local retail stationer to buy a ruled pad and some other things to try to sketch out some ideas on finding a job. He was shocked at the high prices he had to pay. Coming from the highly competitive food store business, he felt that there was an opportunity here for a highly competitive chain of retail office products stores. He did a bit of research and found that the office products business was a highly fragmented industry with lots of small players and tremendous inefficiencies masked by high profit margins at all levels, manufacturing, wholesaling, and retailing.

So Tom went out, got a few backers, and opened his first Staples store and the rest is history, as they say. Today, Staples is over a $16 billion company with approximately 1,780 stores across the country as well as more in Europe. They also have a strong contract division and, after buying our company, a strong mail order division.

Since Staples started, more than 10,000 office supply stores have disappeared along with a good many contract stationers who couldn't compete. Staples worked on lower margins, forced the manufacturers to work on lower margins, and in those instances when it does buy from wholesalers, forced them to work on lower margins. Today, they are even bypassing manufacturers and importing goods under their own label directly from China, Japan, or wherever they can get the best deals.

Early on at Quill, we began selling items under our own label so we could buy for less. The manufacturers all fought this, saying that their brands were more important. Over the years, our Quill brand became the third most a recognized "national" brand. Today, most of the industry carries a huge number of private label products, and the manufacturers are in a much weaker position. Some have gone out of business. It's sort of fun to see how the private label revolution that we started in our industry back in the Sixties has played out.

The irony of all this is that 50 years and more before Tom came on the scene, there were two multiple store office products chains in Chicago: Horders and Utility. Each had eight to 10 stores in the downtown area. Either one could easily have expanded nationwide and have done the same thing Tom did with Staples. But they didn't. Evidently, it never occurred to them that the market was as big as Tom found out it was, that they could really capture a big chunk of it by becoming highly efficient, and they could sell at major discounts.

In fact, in those days, discounting was frowned on by the office products association and by most dealers. We were ostracized in the industry when we first started publishing discount prices, and some manufacturers wouldn't sell to us. (Remember that when you start breaking the rules, your job isn't to be liked. Your job is to be a great business.) But when Tom came in, he changed the rules on the retail side. Utility stores had long since disappeared and Horders followed suit.

I think that this whole concept of changing the rules was best put forth by an economist by the name of Joseph Schumpeter in the early 1900s. He developed a theory called "creative destruction," which set forth the idea that "the vital force behind capitalism is innovation and the entrepreneur willing to introduce it." His theory was that innovations were responsible for both the progress and the instabilities of capitalism.

For Schumpeter, "creative destruction" was a process in which new technologies, new kinds of products, new methods of production, and new means of distribution make old ones obsolete, forcing existing companies to quickly adapt or to fail.

Schumpeter was a big supporter of the entrepreneur. He believed that entrepreneurs advance new products, technology, and production methods and provide the impulse for change. As history shows us, older companies run by managers instead of by entrepreneurs, which almost all companies eventually become at some point in their history, often become the victim of change instead of the innovator of it. Proof of this is that just 45 years later, 80 percent of the 1955 Fortune 500 companies were no longer on the list and in fact a number of them are out of business altogether. They were the "victims of takeovers, market changes, inertia or poor management."

What all of this means to you, the entrepreneur, is that you must look for opportunities in change, whether you create it or respond to it. Change is your business ally; without change, there's no reason for you to go into business. Otherwise, who needs you and your business? There's an old Chinese proverb that says "Every change brings an opportunity and a threat." The one thing that is absolutely certain is that there will be change. Back in 500 B.C. a fellow by the name of Heraclitus said "Nothing is permanent but change."

Yet the foolish people of the world are always fighting change. The Luddites in early nineteenth century England went around smashing machinery in factories because they felt it would put people out of work. In the United States the same thing took place later in the same century when the threshing machine was introduced, and for the same reason.

Looking back, the foolishness of this kind of thinking is apparent. Machinery didn't destroy jobs; it created new ones while bringing down prices to the consumer. And, they brought new opportunities with them. You might think that this kind of foolish thinking is gone. Yet today, here in the United States, that same kind of thinking is behind the outcry over the outsourcing of jobs to foreign, lower-cost manufacturers. I don't believe that this will hurt our country. In fact it will help. We can buy goods for less while concentrating on doing those things that we do best. It's the old "division of labor" concept except now on a world stage. People all used to make their own clothing but at some time in the past, they decided that those who were best at making clothing would do that and that others would focus on what they did best, and a method of exchange was worked out. Outsourcing is the same.

How well you can manage change and the challenges it brings will determine how successful you will be. I read something once where the author said, "Time has a way of changing all assets in a business into liabilities. We tend to carry baggage along long after it has fulfilled its purposes." I not only agree with that but I think it is happening faster and faster because technology is changing faster and ideas are communicated faster.

When Tom Stemberg started Staples and began slashing prices, he changed the rules in the office products business. We waited and watched as others jumped in to copy Tom. At one point, there were about 30 imitators, but in the end, only three survived. But they grew quite large, and by February 1990, we decided we had to meet and beat them, where possible on pricing. We already had them beat on service. And we did, as I talked about in a previous chapter.

It took a lot of thought and some time before we got to where we could do it, but we did. The toughest part was the mental adjustment it took. We were accustomed to pricing all products to produce a profit. But the new rules that Tom introduced to the office products business were like those in the grocery business and included loss leaders. Believe me, it was very tough to price copy paper so low that we actually lost money on every sale. And we sold truckloads of copy paper every day. But those sales also brought along sales of more profitable merchandise. In time, we learned the new rules of the game and adapted to them. And they worked just fine. But why weren't we the ones who had introduced them into the office products business? If we had, maybe Tom wouldn't have found such a big fat, happy industry that he invaded and to a large extent conquered. Yes, he changed the rules and why wasn't it us?

And on and on it goes. The rules are always changing and, thanks to technology, they are changing faster than ever. The day is long past when you could do one thing one way and stick with it throughout your business life. A good rule to follow is one I read once. "There is an easier, better and quicker way to do everything and you can't do that by just sticking with the old tried and true."

So my thought about change is that it can be your best friend. If you are looking to start a business, figure out a method or service or product that no one else is offering. If you are already in business, keep looking for ways to make major changes and even some minor ones. Someone once said, "If it ain't broke, don't fix it," but I believe, along with Schumpeter, in the idea of creative destruction. If it "ain't broke" look for a way of breaking it and then making it even better. You should constantly be looking for ways to improve on it before your competition does it for you—and to you. That is the rule of the life of business, and it isn't going to change.

# Chapter 22

# About the Lifelong Learning Process

When I started the business, I knew virtually nothing about office supplies, about the industry, about pricing, or about the competition. I knew something about selling and about advertising. My education started on June 1, 1956, when I started calling on prospects. When Harvey joined me a year and a half later, he had been out of the Navy for a year or two and didn't even have selling experience. From the beginning, it was a constant learning experience. As I said before, we learned from our customers, from constantly questioning our vendors, and from attending every trade show and talking with dealers from other areas of the country who were not, at that time, competitors of ours. We read the trade journals. We learned from our attorneys, our accountant, our banker. Once we got into the mail order mode, we joined the Direct Marketing Association and did the same there. We also joined a local family owned business group, a local business exchange group, and others to interact and learn from people not in our industry.

Everything we learned helped us build the business, helped us shape it. From the day we started until we sold it 43 years later, we learned everything we could about office products, about running a business, about legal matters, and about estate planning (we're still learning about this).

Many, many years ago it was common that someone could learn a trade from their father, work at it their entire lifetime, and pass the knowledge and skills onto their sons with hardly a change. Being a blacksmith in 1845 required, for example, the same basic skills and tools needed in 1800. But those days are long gone. Today, even if you go into the family business, you have to be constantly learning just to keep up with the constant and fast changes in the marketplace, in technology, in the laws, with changing customer needs and wants, and with the changes in your own company as it grows.

And it's only getting more intense. Changes in the marketplace are faster today than just 50 years ago. When I started in business, the marketplace wasn't static, not by a long shot. But change and innovation didn't come flying at me and Harvey as rapidly when we were working out of a converted coal bin, as when we were sitting atop over a half a billion dollar business in the 1990s. We can thank globalization, the Internet, FedEx, changes in logistics, and a lot of other innovations for that.

An entrepreneur who wants to grow his or her business needs a constant flow of information to both stay on top of change and to understand opportunity. They also need a "sounding board," people who can help sort out what at times can feel like information overload and whom you can bounce ideas off.

You just can't make the mistake of "being a turtle." And, as silly as it sounds, it's easy when you run a business. Lots of promising entrepreneurs get so bogged down in the day-to-day work of running a business that they never poke their head out of the shell. They never take the time to learn. And a business owner who isn't constantly striving to learn is soon finding that they are learning how to deal with negative cash flow or, at the most, a stagnant business.

Learning requires a conscious effort. At Quill, we were constantly working at it. Put into your budget going to at least one industry convention or seminar a year. You always get something from the speakers, although, unfortunately, most of them are usually not that great. But mixing with your peers and your vendors on the showroom floor, at the luncheons, is where you really pick up a lot of intelligence about what is going on in the industry and about what others are doing that you might think of incorporating into your business. Gathering intelligence is an important role of the business leader. Sitting with others in your industry over a beer, talking what seems like small talk, is an easy way to gather intelligence.

Talking with your vendors when they come in to visit you is another great source of information. Part of every conversation should start off with, "What's happening in the industry and in the marketplace?" The sharp salespeople, and particularly the owners, have a lot of knowledge and are usually more than willing to share it.

Reading, constant reading, is a must. Trade journals, general business journals, books on business. All play a part in the lifelong learning process.

You should be talking with other businesspeople on a regular basis. They don't have to be in your industry. There's lots to be learned from people running businesses, even if the business is nothing like yours. I became active in a local business association. My brother Arnold became active in a local group of financial officers. Harvey and I became active in a family owned business group. We were getting a constant flow of ideas from all of these activities.

You'll actually find that other business men and women will become some of your best friends. They understand what it's like, the mix of exhilaration and pressure that comes from running a business. Plus, it's amazing how much learning goes on at social gatherings with other businesspeople. Friendships, even casual ones, who are businesspeople are a great source of information. It's important to have these relationships so you can pick up a phone and ask another businessperson's opinion on some issue. And being able to visit someone's facility who is in a similar line of business, even if in a different industry, is a great way to learn.

What packing material are they using? Peanuts? Foam pack? Air bags? What kind of shipping rates do they pay? What is their order entry system like? Do they use checkers or is there some other way of checking to make sure the orders are processed properly without having a dedicated checker? How do they handle past due accounts? On and on the questions go. There are thousands of them and then some more. Someone is always doing something better than you are, and you can learn from them.

But here's the rub: You can't let the learning take away from the work you must do to run a business. It's long hours, running a business. Learning is one of those things you have to do in addition to making sure you always keep current with the day-to-day business. Running and building a great business pretty much rules out what some young people today call and seem to yearn for, "a balanced life."

As we grew, we encouraged the appropriate people within our organization to also invest time in learning. We had a program whereby we paid for anyone in the organization to attend college classes that were related to business as well as those needed to get a degree in the business field. We also paid for MBA programs at night or on Fridays and Saturdays for certain people who had been with us for some time. We figured that by the time they had that much business experience with us, the additional knowledge they got would be very helpful.

Just as an aside, many MBA schools do require that candidates have some business experience before they can be accepted for their programs. Unfortunately, these schools accept experience working with Wall Street firms or consultants as business experience. Very few of those types of candidates have actually had experience in a real business, a manufacturing or distribution business where they really do something other than juggle money or give advice on things that they know little about other than what they have learned in a classroom.

Learning really is a lifelong process for the entrepreneur who really wants to build a very successful company. If you don't get excited about learning how to do better in business, then I'm not sure you've got the makings of an entrepreneur. In this day and age constant change is essential for the entrepreneur who wants to survive. Things are changing too rapidly and will continue to change even more rapidly in the future to stay where you are because, unless you learn and change, you soon won't be where you were.

Therefore, being a good businessperson is a lifelong learning process, and there are a number of ways to do it. Be creative in how you learn. Be committed to learning. Become the very best you are capable of being. It's the path to building an ever more successful business.

# Chapter 23

# The Art of Survival

Up until now, I've talked about how to build a good company. In this chapter and the next, I want to talk about "The Art of Survival" and, on the other side of the coin, "How to Do Almost Everything Wrong."

I was on a panel a few years ago, speaking to large group of entrepreneurs. One of the questions was, "How did you survive the hard times? Is it heart, stubbornness, or will that helps you continue? How do you know when it is time to throw in the towel?"

My response was that, frankly, we hadn't had very many hard times. That's because we always assumed there would be lean times so we never "bet the ranch" on anything. We never took on any additional overhead until we absolutely, positively couldn't continue with what we had. And when we did take on additional overhead, such as building a bigger headquarters, we already had the income to support the new added expense. No, let me correct that: we had the income to do much more than support it. In other words, we never, ever said, "We will do this because we are growing and we know that we will be able to support it." That is a fool's reasoning. Or perhaps an egomaniac's reasoning. But more about that in the next chapter "How to Do Almost Everything Wrong."

Also, we hated debt. I started business in 1956 and I borrowed a small amount of money in 1959 for a very special buy, and paid it back very quickly. Then again in 1962, when we put out our first full line catalog and expanded our warehousing space, although we had the income to do these things, we needed cash to stock many of the items shown in that catalog. They were all bread and butter (or should I say rubberband and paper clip?) items that we knew would sell. So we borrowed about $20,000 to pay for that inventory. We paid the money back on schedule in quarterly payments but had a bad experience with a young, new loan officer who made us hate the experience, so we never again borrowed money to finance the business. We grew to be that $630-million-plus business, all financed by retained earnings.

We controlled our living standards, taking very modest salaries, even when the business grew quite large. We always retained a significant portion, the vast majority of earnings, in the business to fund our growth. Toward the end, when we had far more than we needed in the business in a big reserve fund, we did begin to distribute dividends to the family based on the previous year's profits.

So we never really had hard times, if you define hard times as being threatened with going out of business because of a lack of funds to survive some downturns or mistakes.

One of the smartest, most practical people I know is a lifelong friend who was our corporate accountant from day one, when we were both one man shops. He remained our accountant for about 30 years, when he sold his then 100-person firm and later went into the mergers and acquisitions business. He gave one of the best speeches I've ever heard, and I'm borrowing liberally from it here. He started this speech by saying that during his 30 years of public accounting he had worked with hundreds of entrepreneurs and that by observing them he had learned many of the "do's" and just about all of the "don't's" for surviving and growing. He went on to say that the manager's (entrepreneur's) first obligation is to keep the business alive. There can be no growth without survival. Yet many managers seem to be suicidal.

Then he listed six actual recent examples of "How to Kill a Business."

1. A cash short manufacturer bought, with a floating rate loan, an expensive building, in a foreign country, to house a sales operation that had been doing well in much smaller, less expensive

quarters. Chapter 11 bankruptcy followed. (My comment: why couldn't he have just leased additional space if he really needed it until the volume was built to the point where they could afford it? It's less efficient, but so what?)

2. Despite repeated warnings from bankers and CPAs, a distributor accumulated ever larger inventories, financed by large bank loans. Declining sales and high interest rates created a horrible squeeze. The owners are not sleeping well. (My comment: inventories can kill you. This is particularly true when you let some merchandise slip into the obsolete zone. I believe you are much better off getting rid of obsolete merchandise as quickly as you can, at whatever price you can get for it. And certainly, they should never be carried on the books at full value. This gives you a false picture of your profitability. Further, you should always be working for slim inventories and very high inventory turns. Forget the extra discounts manufacturers offer you for quantities larger than you need. What is an extra 10 percent off when you could be forced into not discounting your bills? As I have pointed out if a manufacturer gives you 1 percent 10, net 30-day terms, you make 18.25 percent by paying your bills 20 days early since there are 18.25 20-day periods in a year. That's 36.50 percent savings if the terms are 2 percent 10 days, net 30. Inventory turns are as critical to a business as good blood circulation is to a human. You almost never save that much in larger quantity purchases.)

3. A successful business was neglected for the nearly fatal pursuit of other activities. (My comment: as long as we had Quill, my brothers and I had a laserlike focus on the company. It took almost all of our time and energy. While we contributed to various charitable causes, we never got deeply involved with any except for City of Hope, which was a cause that the industry had adopted as its own. There will be plenty of time after you retire to get involved with charities and other such activities. And if you focus on your business during your working career,

you'll have a lot more money to give to the charities or to fund other activities you like.)

4. A partner was bought out by the business. A new store was also opened, at great cost, for inventory and improvements. The bank finally refused to provide the necessary loans and the business was in trouble. (My comment: one thing at a time and only what you can really afford to do. Something may look good in the long term. But you always have to remember that you have to survive the short term in order for there to be a long term.)

5. After a substantial drop in sales, a wholesaler cut expenses "to the bone," but not fast enough. Finally, in chapter 11, bankruptcy, further cuts were so great that the company started to earn more than at any time in its history. (My comment: Companies always, always accumulate waste, far more than you can possibly imagine. Reread Chapter 14, "You Can, Too, Argue with Success.")

6. The CPAs and lawyers prospered because three families battled over control of a manufacturing business. The expenditure of time and money may prove fatal. (My comment: Human nature being what it is, I have no idea of how to avoid these kinds of conflicts. All I can say is that my brothers and I got along so well that people often commented on it. One of the secrets was that we all felt that if the business prospered then we would all be much better off. So the welfare of the business came first. Also, all of our wives stayed out of business affairs. Even though my late wife worked there part-time, she did not get involved in business decisions. She did her job, in her area. The same was true of the children when they worked at the company. My brothers and I each were responsible for a certain segment of the business, and we each ran our own portions, but with a lot of communication and sharing of ideas between us. Fortunately, we three had the same values, including the hard work ethic. It worked well for us. Also, although we never had to use

them, we wrote all our agreements, Buy-Sell, and so on on the supposition that if it came to disagreements, we might battle one another. And we had it all in writing, so each of us felt secure. That, I believe, helped make things easier.)

7. Harassed and overworked management often results from trying to do too much. Management resources are limited in *all* companies. To grow strong, a company must use its management in endeavors for which:

   - Risk is reasonable.

   - Profit opportunity is significant relative to competing endeavors.

   - Management has the required skills and motivation.

My friend went on in his speech to list six Keys to Survival. Here they are.

1. Take no action that may jeopardize survival.

   - Applies even if the proposed action may produce a large benefit.

   - Exception: the business risked is no great loss, and the owner doesn't much care anyway.

2. Recognize that your resources (mainly capital and management) are limited and allocate them only to the most effective uses. In difficult times, fewer balls can be kept in the air.

3. Plan your work and work your plan. A detailed monthly budget or projection must be prepared. With proper analysis and attention you should be able to determine necessary expense levels and allocation of resources. Computer spreadsheet programs make this a relatively easy task.

4. Get a dependable source of finance and be a dependable source of repayment. Don't need more than can be *conservatively* repaid. (My comment: The best source of finance is retained earnings.)

5. Pursue growth. There is more to survival than circling the wagons, even when such circling is required. Survival requires growth and planning for growth. (My comment: If you don't grow, others will and will soon go after your customers for even more growth. And they will have become stronger than you. Besides, markets keep changing and you have to change and grow as they do. We experienced that in our office products market.)

6. Curb your ego, the strong conviction that you can accomplish absolutely anything is a firm foundation upon which to build disaster. (My note: I couldn't agree more. More about this in the next chapter "How to Do Almost Everything Wrong." Also, just because you are successful at one thing does not mean you can be successful at other things. Most very successful businesspeople know their industry, their market, and their company very well as a result of years of hard work and experience in that particular arena. But they are babes in the woods in another setting. Let being a success in your own business in your own industry satisfy your ego. It certainly will satisfy your pocketbook.)

Finally, my friend in his speech said, "If a business closes, all employees lose their jobs, creditors lose business and all or most of their receivables, and the owner loses his life's work. Abhorrent as it is to most business owners, Chapter 11 can be a last ditch survival technique to save employees, creditors and the owner. There are times when radical surgery is necessary to save a life."

So that is what my friend had to say about The Art of Survival. He is a very wise man, and his business advice served us well over the years. I think we can all agree that surviving is a good thing and failing is a bad thing. To survive, and then to survive well, is a primary goal for all entrepreneurs. It trumps high living, ego, and just about all else you can think of except honor, integrity, and a few other such values.

# Chapter 24

# How to Do Almost Everything Wrong

As I have said, I often reflect on one of my father's laments. "Oh," he would say, referring to my brothers and me, "if you guys could only learn from my mistakes." He meant, of course, that if we could learn from his mistakes, we wouldn't have to repeat them and suffer the consequences. But in a broader sense, he was questioning how much people learn from others' experiences.

Actually, I did learn a lot from some of Dad's mistakes and they helped me a great deal in my own life. So while I share some of his skepticism about learning from the past and the mistakes of others (as well as the successes), I am optimistic that you can truly learn from my blunders and of others. The biggest problem is that, all too often, we don't bother to look back. We don't study what happened in the past. Or as George Santayana, the philosopher, poet, and essayist once wrote, "Those who cannot remember the past are condemned to repeat it."

So with that in mind, I begin this chapter on "how to do almost everything wrong!" Let me tell you some stories first. I've already mentioned them but now let's see what we really did wrong. They are interesting just by themselves and should make for a good, quick read. Then I tell you what I think the important lessons are.

Recall that at one time, my brothers and I felt that we could increase our growth rate by really getting into the office furniture business. We already were selling about $20 million of furniture through our catalog, but we were not tapping into the biggest share of the office furniture business, the contract furniture area, where you would design and outfit whole offices.

So we bought a failing chain of office furniture stores in the Chicago area. We knew nothing about retail, and we had limited experience with outside salespeople. We had started our company on the street selling, but we converted to mail order very early. Thus, we were getting way outside our field of expertise. We promptly followed that mistake by putting one of our buyers, who had some retail experience, in charge. The company continued to lose money. Then we hired someone with some more experience in retailing, but none in office furniture. That didn't work.

Finally, I personally took over, splitting my time between mail order Quill and office furniture Quill. After all, I was successful at mail order Quill so I should be able to be successful at office furniture Quill. Right?

Wrong. I couldn't get it turned around and I was getting exhausted trying. I'm sure it cost our mail order in lost opportunities because I was so involved in the retail furniture division. Our board of advisors insisted that we give it up. And although they were only advisors and not directors as in a public company, we gave up on it and sold it at a loss.

The second misadventure we had was when we tried to go into Canada. Our chief mail order competitor in the United States had established himself successfully in Europe and was growing well there. (Eventually his European arm became bigger than his U.S. arm.) So we figured we should start to venture outside the United States and we began studying both Mexico and Canada. Mexico scared us for a number of reasons but Canada looked more like the United States so we decided to start there. We set up a distribution center in Toronto and began mailing our flyers and catalogs with Canadian pricing.

We began getting a positive response but we just couldn't seem to break into the profit column. After three or four years, we closed down that operation and returned to focusing just on the United States where we continued to do very well.

But why weren't we successful in Canada? In the first place, we didn't understand Canada, its geography and its makeup. We didn't fully realize that Canada is about 5,000 miles wide from ocean to ocean and about one mile north to south. All that expanse of land you see on the map is not very well populated, except by animals. And believe me it's awfully tough to give really good service over 5,000 miles from just one distribution center.

And then, we didn't fully realize that Canada is really two countries, not one. The French in Quebec are very into themselves, their language, and their culture. You couldn't even do a mailing into Quebec unless it was in the French language. And then, every product had to have French on the label. One of our strengths was our private label line and it would have been prohibitive to redo all our packaging to try to capture the Quebec market. So we gave up trying to sell in Quebec.

We had realized that Canada was only 10 percent of the U.S. market, but we had not realized how spread out that 10 percent was and how divided it was between the English-speaking section and the French-speaking section.

So what were our mistakes in Canada? First and foremost, we didn't invest in enough good, qualified research. Second, we put some of our people from the United States in charge of running the distribution center there. But more importantly, with their help, we tried to do all the marketing from our U.S. headquarters. We did not seek out and hire a top Canadian office products person to run that whole operation, including the marketing.

Finally, we pulled out too fast. We had the resources and the profit flow from our U.S. operation necessary to make the Canadian operation a success. But, being unaccustomed to losing money, and, perhaps rightly, figuring that we could use the same resources better in the United States, we just decided to close the operation down. We sold it to a competitor at something of a loss and ended that venture.

Since selling Quill, I have had two other experiences with businesses, one a start-up and the other a more established company. In each of them, there were things being done that doomed them to failure in the case of one, and near failure in the case of the other.

The first, the start-up, was the brainchild of a very successful and smart individual who had made his fortune in the computer consulting business. He had the idea that he could develop a program to help modernize teaching. His goal was partly financial gains and partly the desire to do some good. His product would help teachers develop lesson plans, and he would create an interactive database so teachers could share their plans with other teachers across the country. Homework assignments could be put on the Internet so students could access them from home as could their parents so no kid could say, "I don't have any homework today." And there was much more to the program.

A second stage was to be the development of a program for use by the administration to comply with all the state required reporting and record keeping. But in the beginning all the effort and money would be put into the first stage.

To raise money, my friend went to individuals who were capable of investing. My brother and I were two who invested—in the first stage investment, in the second stage investment, and even in the third stage investment, until the company went under. There was a private equity fund that also invested as well as the founder himself.

The founder bought a building to house this new enterprise and hired topflight computer gurus as well as others in administration and sales. It looked like a real honest to goodness company with lots of people working very hard to develop the programs and others talking to schools about what they thought was needed. Unfortunately, while the programmers were professionals, the others were amateurs. They certainly found out what many teachers felt they needed in such a program, and they developed the program. What they didn't find out was that many teachers, and their unions, would block the installation of such a program because some teachers weren't computer literate and would be at a disadvantage. Many teachers felt threatened by this new tool.

There was no way this small company had the resources to win acceptance in enough schools to make this a viable enterprise. At every board meeting we got glowing reports of how well accepted the program was at this and that school district. Projections were made about trials, conversion rates, and future income streams. At the same time, we kept getting reports about our "burn rate," in other words, how fast we were burning through our cash and when we would need another round of financing, further diluting our ownership in the company. Well, the trials often didn't happen, and when they did, for the reasons stated, the conversion rates and income streams didn't happen. But the burn rate (a term I never want to hear again) continued until the firm finally closed down.

There were a number of things that were done wrong. In the first place, the firm was started and staffed with people who did not know and did not understand the market they were targeting. The second mistake was that they developed this fancy business plan and committed money to it as if it were the unquestionable truth. A third mistake was that when things weren't happening according to plan, the plan wasn't aggressively revisited, or at least not soon enough to save the company. Another major mistake was in picking the wrong target for the start-up phase.

The administration program would have had a much better chance to succeed. In the first place, administrators were buried under a load of record keeping and reporting requirements. There was a very viable, obvious need. Also, the administration could make its own decisions without having to involve numerous teachers and their unions. Finally, all of the people in administration offices were computer literate.

So a good idea failed, literally burning millions of dollars in the process.

Let me tell you now about the other business, the somewhat more established business. I mentioned it earlier in Chapter 14 when I talked about cutting costs. I want to tell you more about it in this chapter, about how they did almost everything wrong except the product and the service. It had a great product line, one that I really love. When I first became involved, financially, they were in one of their usual financial difficulties. Over the next few years, I got more and more involved and was continually being amazed at how many incredibly stupid mistakes had been made over the years.

The founder is an extremely nice guy, a motivational speaker, and one of the world's leading optimists. And that last was his undoing. From what I could tell, there was never an idea he didn't like. The business started as a mail order company and then, with no experience in any of the areas, they quickly expanded into franchising, company owned stores (with long leases), a golf catalog, and an overseas venture.

They did all of this without the organization, the finances, or the experience and expertise to make it happen. Then, to top it all off, they believed their own projections, so, of course, they needed a very nice headquarters and manufacturing and shipping facility to handle all this business that was going to begin pouring in. So they had one built to their (long in the future, if ever) needs and signed an expensive, long-term lease.

Along the way, to raise money and because it was the "thing to do" for a growing and future great company, they went public. That, in my opinion is one of the dumbest things a small company (even a large one, in my opinion) could do. They immediately added about $500,000 to their expenses to do all the reporting, and so on that a public company must do plus hundreds, if not thousands, of hours of management time wasted dealing with stockholders, required reports, stock holder meetings, and answering stockholders' questions and complaints.

And, of course, because they were going to be so big, they built a management structure for a big company. When I got involved with the company, they had a president and six vice presidents. A $45 million company with six vice presidents! Most of them, by the way, relatively inexperienced and all of them with relatively expensive severance packages. After all, that's what the big companies do.

The founder, probably wisely, had decided he was not a good administrator and hired a president. Being a public company, one destined for great things, he felt, the president got a pretty good package of benefits and severance provisions. That president pushed the company into some ill-considered ventures that lost the company even more money and eventually he was gone. The next president was someone who knew mail order but nothing about retail or franchising and, frankly, not all that much about mail order.

Also, he was very conservative and risk adverse to a fault. His whole management team became the same way. Nothing was done unless there was that 120 percent chance of success, guaranteed. And, of course, in business there is no such thing as that. So the company went along pretty much in the same vein as before. Financial crisis after financial crisis kept the company heavily in debt to a bank that took on such risky loans and always demanded its pound of flesh.

As I got more involved, more and more skeletons tumbled out of the closets as each new door was opened. The company had cosigned on some retail leases. Franchisees were not being charged the full cost of freight because they were complaining about the difficulty they were having making money. Being a public company, they—of course!—felt that they had to have one of the largest, most expensive accounting firms. To that firm, this company was peanuts and items in the statements that were critical to show the true state of affairs were mere footnotes, if that, to this firm. After switching to a smaller accounting firm that dealt with such companies, it took several years to uncover all the irregularities.

Well, after a few years of investing in the company, being on the board and then becoming chairman of the board, we weren't able to improve very much on the performance, and we put it up for sale.

We found only one buyer and he wanted to buy it at a ridiculously low price and would do so only if I stayed on and kept my investment in the company. I decided at that price and under those conditions, I might as well buy it all myself. Frankly, from a personal viewpoint, that wasn't too smart. Suddenly, after selling a business we took 43 years to build, I was back in business. Not a smart thing to do if you want to enjoy your retirement.

Once I bought it, I took it private and cut the number of vice presidents from six to two. And in about a year, we cut out those two. A small company doesn't need a lot of vice presidents. Of course, with the severance packages they had, that cost a bit of money. Also, I decided to let the president go and promoted the chief financial officer into the presidency. He wasn't a mail order guy, but he was smart, hard working, had a lot of integrity and a good deal of business experience. He also had the guts to tell me all the things that were wrong with the company. Also, since I had so much experience with business to business mail order, I felt I could act as the mail order and marketing consultant to him by putting in two or three days a month plus daily phone conferencing, we could make it work.

My idea was probably right, but I soon learned a painful lesson. At Quill, we had a product line that had thousands of items, items that customers needed. So once you got a new customer, the repeat business was great. In this business, it wasn't so much of a "need" product line as a "nice to have" type product line. And the repeat factor was very low, with most customers buying just once or twice a year instead of weekly, monthly, or even more often. There was a whole different tempo to this business, and it took me a while to realize that.

The retail stores we owned were losing money and were taking a lot of management time, so we decided to close them all down. It cost us a lot to buy our way out of many of the leases. Our franchises were also taking a lot of management time and were always demanding more and more. They were also using us as a bank, many of them not paying their bills on time. We cut all the slow pay accounts off and told the rest that they should realize that they were in business for themselves, and we let them handle other product lines. We continued to live up to our franchise agreements and supply product at the wholesale cost. But that was it.

So our focus was now strictly on the business to business mail order side. It took me a long time to realize that the tempo of this business was different from Quill's. But once I did, we decided that we could not pay a tremendous amount for new customers. So we cut our prospecting down to just those prospects who responded well and where we could acquire new customers at a cost that we could recover quickly on their slow repeat business. We cut our prospect mailings by more than 60 percent and, much to our delight, we found that we were getting almost as much business as before.

In addition to that $500,000 savings by becoming private and not having to comply with all kinds of publicly traded "stuff," we also found another several million dollars in savings by doing things better, smarter. Believe me, there's always a lot of waste that can be cut out. Without retail and with fewer demands from franchisees, we were able to make even more cuts in staffing.

To make a long story short, we cut the size of the company and we are finally beginning to make money. We have a way to go to pay off the bank loan and to make us a great business, but the signs look good.

The point of all this is that it takes a long time and a lot of effort to become good at something. Your post experience may help speed up the learning, but it is still going to take time.

Also, once again, don't believe that your business plans will work as you have laid them out, and certainly don't bet the farm on your projections. Don't say, "Gee, we're going to become very big so let's prepare for it," and then commit yourself to some big, fixed expenses.

It's not so bad to dream big but wait until you achieve that "bigness" before you make some expensive long-term commitments. Being overcrowded and being a little less efficient is not such a bad thing for awhile.

And so back to Dad's comment, "If you guys could only learn from my mistakes," and Santayana's dictum, "Those who cannot remember the past are condemned to repeat it." I don't want to end this chapter without some comments on lessons learned. Some of these lessons are in other chapters, but these eight are worth repeating here because they bear on the examples just given.

1. *Moving outside of one's core competency.* This is truly a recipe for disaster, almost always. It stems from the belief that one is invincible and that nothing can go wrong. This belief usually comes from some past (or current) success. It's the false notion that says, "Gee, if we are good at this, then we can be good at anything." That is almost always a false belief.

2. *Trying to cover all bases.* It is truly amazing how limited most of us, even the most successful, are in our abilities. Most respected business people are good at one or two very important elements of their businesses. The best of them realize this and get very good people to handle the other aspects. In the examples in this chapter, this proved to be true. By trying to do things for which they had no expertise and not bringing in people with the expertise in those areas, those ventures were doomed.

3. *Betting the farm.* Sometimes, people get so sold on a premise that they risk everything to pursue it. It sounds heroic, and some great business success stories may show that it *sometimes* works. But it is almost always a foolish move. When you are first starting, there may be no choice. But once a business is established, you don't bet the farm. Most plans and projections don't work out exactly as laid out or as quickly as expected. You have to be prepared and capable of retreating, making adjustments and moving ahead. But, if you've bet the farm, you've lost.

4. *Striving for rapid growth.* Most businesses, contrary to some of the super success stories you read about, start humbly and grow slowly. Read about the early days of most of the large companies (not high-tech companies that rocketed in the tech boom) and you'll find they experienced slow steady growth. Constant yearly, digestible growth (in sales and profits) increases over

25 years or so become a very big number. There's nothing wrong with consistent 7 percent, 10 percent, 15 percent growth rates. The power of compounding is truly amazing. Besides, when that is your pattern, you don't get tempted by grandiose ideas and don't take on great, unneeded overhead in anticipation of very rapid success.

5. *Counting on a limitless fountain of money.* There just is no such thing. As my accountant friend once said, "Strive to make a profit every year, even if it is just one dollar." Losing money year after year, always believing that success is just around the corner is not the road to success. On the other hand, pulling the plug too soon on a new venture when it is losing money could be a mistake, as long as the rest of the operation can sustain the losses and still be profitable.

6. *Not clearing out the dead wood fast enough is a major error.* This applies all up and down the corporate ladder. Only a hard driving, committed, unified team with the right talents can lead to great success.

7. *Know your business, your customers, and the marketplace.* When you start small and put in the time and effort to learn about all of these, you can make it even in an unfamiliar industry. I did. But when you jump into it and commit large amounts of money to it, the losses can be staggering, if not fatal.

8. *Don't blindly follow your advisors, either from inside or from outside the company.* They have their own agendas, their own prejudices, their own weak spots. They are there to give different insights and opinions, which you take into account when making your decision. And you should pay very careful attention. But, in the end, it has to be your decision to live or die by.

The list could go on and on. The point of this whole chapter is that a critical study of the history of companies, successful ones and failed ones, could help a lot of businesspeople avoid the pain of repeating many of these mistakes. The daily papers and the business magazines are replete with such stories that are happening every day. Take those lessons to heart, and don't feel that you are so much smarter than those who led those failing companies. You're probably not.

But then, of course, each generation feels invincible and incredibly smarter than their predecessors, particularly when they are holding that piece of paper (that MBA from a big-name school) that says so.

# Chapter 25

# About Advisors and Boards

Critical to your success as an entrepreneur is good advice. And there's lots of good advice to go around. The problem is that most businesspeople don't take advantage of all the advice that is out there.

Your accountant, your banker, your lawyer(s), and your insurance agent are just a few of the advisors available to you. They are your first line advisors, and you should use them for more than just the bare bones tasks. Unfortunately, most entrepreneurs don't.

As I have mentioned, when I first started in business, my best friend was just starting his own accounting firm so he became my accountant. Let me give you just a few pieces of the advice he gave to us over the years that resulted in tremendous benefits for us. The first came when we wanted to add a benefits program for our employees. He absolutely advised against a defined benefits program, whereby you contract to pay certain retirement benefits to your employees sometime in the future. This, he said, becomes an underfunded liability that could really hurt us. And today, almost 50 years later, look at all the industries such as the automobile industry, the steel industry, the airlines industry, and many more that are in trouble because of the huge cost of their underfunded defined benefits program. (And then, of course, there are the defined benefits plans called Social Security, Medicare, and Medicaid which are on the verge of going bust.)

He advised us to go into a defined contribution (profit sharing) plan, whereby each year we would deposit a certain percentage of our profits into a separate fund that belonged to the employees, which they would get when they left the company or retired. (As I mentioned earlier, one of our warehouse people who had been with us for more than 35 years retired with almost a million dollars in his profit sharing fund.) The beauty of the program was that once we made the payment into the fund at year end, we had no further liability.

Also, of course, in the beginning, it was a great benefit for us because the bosses' salaries were a major part of the salaries paid and so a good portion of the profit sharing payment flowed into our accounts. But that didn't last long. At the end, the portion of the contribution that went into our accounts was almost an infinitesimal part of the contribution. But we were very happy that we had such a program because we used it as a tool to keep everyone focused on doing everything possible to keep growing the profits.

Another great piece of advice was that we become an S corporation instead of a C corporation so that we wouldn't have to be double taxed first on profits and then on dividends if we ever got to the point where we wanted to declare them. Much later on in our corporate life, this paid off big time.

One more among many more pieces of advice he gave us was that when we wanted to buy real estate for our business, that we buy it personally and not have the company own it. As the years went by and I talked to other entrepreneurs, it was amazing to me how many of them had purchased their property through the company. To us, this single piece of advice became worth an amazing amount of money personally and actually launched us into the real estate business after we sold the company. Our accountant's advice was very critical in how we were able to maximize our returns from the business.

Yet, many businesspeople use their accountants just to prepare a financial statement once a year and then just look at the bottom line to see how much they made or lost without going over that statement line by line with their accountant and other top people in the company to see what might be improved. What a waste of a great source of advice. Meeting with an accountant is rarely the social highlight of the season. But when it comes to understanding your business, how you make money (or lose money), and what very tangible steps you can take to make more, meeting with your accountant and getting a clear explanation of your financial statements is one of the most productive meetings you'll ever have. In my opinion, it's a must for every business owner.

Over the years we also spent a good deal of time keeping our banker up-to-date on what we were doing and what we planned to do. I shared earlier in the book about how I met my first banker. He was a loan officer at a medium-sized bank in Chicago. I first went in to introduce myself, showing him that balance sheet of a bit of cash and a used car. And my first financial statement for the first month I was in business showed sales of $960 and profits of $35 (with no salary, of course). He took the time to talk to me, and he took an interest in what I was trying to do. Then, after he retired, the bank was sold, and we transferred to another, much larger bank, we continued to see our contact every month to show him our financial statement and chat about what we were doing.

The bank we eventually settled with also became an important partner. You really want your bank to be your partner, to have an interest in your business, in how you are doing. You want them to understand your business, to understand you and your goals. To make that happen, you have to work at it. You have to keep them informed, the good and the bad and keep them honestly informed. Most bankers have seen it all and take projections and promises with a great many grains of salt.

Remember, keeping your banker informed, giving him/her your financial statement, good or bad, every month, keeping them up-to-date on your plans, your successes and your failures, is the best way there is to make them a partner in your business. They can help with advice, with contacts, and when needed, with money. Just imagine when the day comes when you need an influx of capital to grab the largest opportunity yet to present itself to you. Wouldn't you feel better if you had a first-name relationship with your banker, someone who understood not only your business today but your goals for tomorrow, someone who believed in you because they knew you well and knew what you were doing?

Another usually underutilized advisor is your lawyer(s). In to-day's world, they have become more important than ever. But most beginning entrepreneurs rarely look to their lawyer for advice. They may use the lawyer for filing incorporation papers and such, but then they tend to forget the lawyer's number. When I started in business in 1956 it was just a matter of drawing up the paper-work to form the Sub S corporation. But as time went on and we became larger and larger, we were turning to our attorneys for more and more advice. Of course, our society was becoming more and more litigious at the same time, so there was all the more reason for us to be consulting our attorneys.

This was particularly true in the employee relations field. Somewhere along the line, we hired a law firm specializing in labor relations on a retainer basis just to deal with the problems and potential problems that could arise in that area. Fighting off union organizing attempts was just one area they helped in. We had just one major unionizing attempt and with the lawyers' advice and with a lot of hard work, we won that battle—by a huge margin. (That wasn't too hard to do because we paid better and had better benefits than similar organizations with unions. And we treated our people well, which is always a must-do for every busi-ness.) But where our labor attorneys were really needed was in the ordinary course of business, the training of our supervisors and, most importantly, when it came to firing someone. No matter how good the cause, in this day and age, if you don't do it right, you can be sued for discrimination of one sort or another. So their advice became critical.

Another area where the advice of attorneys was critical was in the estate planning area. The best time to begin your estate plan-ning is when your business is small and growing. At that stage, it's relatively inexpensive to transfer ownership shares (nonvoting, of course) on to the next generation. Then as the company grows, those shares become more and more valuable and, between gift taxes and/or death taxes, very costly to pass on. It amazes me how many successful businesspeople have failed to do estate planning. I guess, being the optimists that entrepreneurs are, they imagine that they will live forever.

Actually, although we used attorneys a lot, we were involved in only two lawsuits in our entire 43 years in business. The first was when we sued someone for using our trademarked name. We won. The second suit was with the state of North Dakota when they claimed that we, an out-of-state company with no physical presence (Nexus is the legal term) in North Dakota, had to collect tax on the sales in their state. We fought that one all the way up to the U.S. Supreme Court and won. It was the one and only time I have seen the Supreme Court in action. But they were the most expensive seats we had ever bought. It cost us more than a million dollars, but we just simply refused to give in on something in which we felt we were right.

Thus your banker, your accountant, your lawyers are all good sources for advice. If you pick good ones, they have probably been down the road before and have a lot of knowledge that will help you avoid problems and can help broaden your own thinking. Picking someone only because they are a friend (or relative) is a stupid thing to do. Your business success may depend on their advice. So choose carefully and wisely.

This brings me to one other source of good advice: a board of advisors. In a public company, they are called a board of directors because they can wield real power, hiring and firing presidents, and so on. But in a private company, they are simply advisors.

We didn't create a board of advisors until the latter years that we were in business, and that was our loss. We should have done it earlier. But when we did, we did it right. Many entrepreneurs put their lawyers, accountants, or bankers, or, worse still, some personal friend on their boards. We didn't do that. Those folks are already being paid for their advice and help. They had too much to lose if they started telling you that you were wrong.

We wanted honest to goodness, hard-nosed advice about what we were doing right and should do more of, and what we were doing wrong. So we looked for people who could really help us grow the company larger and run it better, without some other agenda interfering with the advice they gave.

And we built just such a board. We had a CEO from a larger, and very well run distribution company, a chief financial officer from a company that was four or five times our size, a very sharp, tough entrepreneurial guy who ran an interesting business, and a woman who was an outstanding consultant in the areas of employee relations and organizational structure, particularly in large family businesses. We met quarterly and provided each of them with our last quarterly financial statements along with commentary several weeks before the meetings. We paid them the going rate for board members (plus all expenses) and paid for telephone conferences or special meetings between the quarterly board meetings.

We got more than our money's worth. None of them were bashful about telling us things we were doing wrong and should change. These folks all had a lot of very good experience, could put things in the proper perspective, and could come up with some great suggestions. I advise every entrepreneur to set up a very good board of advisors as soon as they can possibly afford it—or sooner.

There are a lot of ways to get very good advice that will help you become successful—or even more successful. It isn't an easy thing to accomplish but it's a heck of a lot easier and cheaper than making some of the dumb mistakes you can make without that kind of advice.

# Chapter 26

# A Family Business Can Be
# Great—or . . .

Family businesses can be great, bringing the family closer together, creating wealth for the entire family, and much more—or they can be disasters, tearing families apart and wasting wonderful opportunities for creating great wealth and doing good things.

There is a great deal of material on family businesses and on how families can work together without killing each other. In fact, a whole industry has sprung up giving advice on family businesses and on families working together. There are even family business associations that spend a good part of their time covering this topic. What follows in this chapter is not based on a lot of study and research, unless you call 43 years working with one brother and 25 years working with two brothers lots of study and research! I do, of course. Plus, I've seen a lot of other family businesses up close.

I can't imagine how our experience could have been better. In addition to the three of us, most of our kids were in the business at one time or another. And again, it worked out very well. Unfortunately, none of our kids had a desire to run the business. It would have been nice to see the business go on to the next generation, but we're not that unhappy that it didn't. The industry had changed a great deal and it is good to see everyone able to pursue their own interests. Besides, my observation is that all family businesses eventually get sold, go public (which is a sale), or go out of business. It's just a question of which generation does it. Mostly it's the first generation who does it. Few family businesses last to the second generation, very few to the third, and an infinitesimal number beyond that.

So how did we do it? How did we go through all those years, working together, building together, and still remain, not just talking to each other but "best friends?"

I would say that the first thing that made this possible was that we all had the same values. In fact, if different family members have different values, it is highly unlikely that they can continue to work well together. Our values looked like this:

- We all worked hard. Never once did any of us feel that either of the other two was slacking off.

- We all had the same sense of honesty and integrity. This was important because we presented a united front to our employees and our customers in this area. They knew they could rely on us and trust us, and we knew we could rely on one another and trust one another.

- There were never any arguments about control or about money. I started the firm and I always held on to 51 percent of the voting stock. Harvey, who joined me a year-and-a-half later, had 49 percent of the voting stock. Arnold, who joined us 25 years later, had a quantity of nonvoting stock. But I never, ever exercised my controlling stock. When there was a major issue or major decision to be made, we discussed it among ourselves until we all agreed on a course of action. Not one of us had less say than the others. If we couldn't agree, we didn't take action.

- What made this requirement for unanimity work was that we all were reasonable people and we all had the interest of the business at heart. All felt that the welfare of the business came first because all good things would flow from a successful business. If the business was healthy, strong, and profitable, then we would all benefit from that.

- We genuinely liked and respected one another. We could be in a meeting with 10 to 15 of our people and argue forcefully with one another. I was usually the one who would blow up and really get agitated about something, and Harvey was the one who would try to inject some pacifying thoughts into the discussion. Arnold, who could also blow up on occasion, was usually the quietest of the three of us. What amazed people who witnessed some of these sessions was that after the meeting was over, the three of us would go to lunch together as if there had never been a serious blowup just a few minutes earlier. I think this was possible because the blowup was always about some business issue, never about a personal issue. So once the meeting was over, whether we had settled the matter or not, we were back in our brotherly relationship.

- There were never any arguments about money. As soon as Harvey joined me, our salaries, small as they were at that time, were the same and that continued throughout our business relationship. When Arnold joined us, his salary, while less than ours, was a good salary. Later, it was raised to more closely match ours. But in spite of that salary difference and the ownership difference, when we needed a new corporate headquarters and we purchased land and built our building, financed on the strength of Quill's long-term lease, we all had equal one-third interests. This continued when we did other real estate deals backed by the strength of Quill. The real estate became a real source of both income and wealth that we and our families all shared equally. Money never became an issue between us.

- When any of our children joined the business, they were paid based on the jobs they had. Their pay and bonuses were the same as others working in the same position and with the same performance. There was only one incident when one of my nephews demanded a big promotion and a salary he didn't deserve and quit when I wouldn't give it to him. That caused his mother to get mad at me and stop talking to me for many years. Later we got back onto good terms. But my brother was smart enough to never bring that into the business and it never became an issue.

- This brings up another major reason for our harmonious relations. Our wives never, ever interfered in the business. Whatever any of them may have said to their husbands never got back to the business. My wife, once the kids were in high school, decided she wanted to go back to work, and she took a position in the advertising department. But even though she was working in the business, she never wanted to, nor tried to, insert herself into business decisions. She worked at her job and had the same responsibilities as anyone else in that position. All too often, spouses get involved where they shouldn't, either at home or if they work in the business, and spark problems. Of course, these days many women own and run businesses, and it is the husbands who should be careful not to interfere.

- We all had different strengths and we carved up responsibilities between us based on those strengths. Arnold, who was a CPA, was a financial whiz and a good people person. He handled all the accounting, credit, and personnel areas. Harvey was a very good detail guy. He handled the operations side of the business. My strength was in advertising, merchandising, and marketing and that is where I concentrated. This is one of the most important elements in having a successful family business relationship. Divide responsibilities and each individual runs his/her area.

- A very important part of carving up of responsibilities is communication. Good communication is always one area in a business that everyone complains about. Every employee always feels there is a lack of good communication. Each one seems to feel that they should know everything that is going on in the company. And that just isn't so. Everyone doesn't need to know everything. But we found that although we each had our own areas of the business to run, constantly communicating with one another about what was going on in our various areas, what problems there were, what we were thinking about, and so on, was the grease that really kept everything running very smoothly. There were seldom, if ever, any surprises.

The point is, we each had different strengths and it wasn't until we figured out that each of us should be responsible for different areas of the business based on our individual expertise (always keeping the other two up-to-date on what was taking place) that we really had a smooth operation. Before that, we kept getting into each other's way and kept having some issues. Once we settled on the clear separation of responsibilities, which happened early in the game, things went exceedingly well. Our biggest feuds then became things like what color wallpaper we were going to use in the executive washroom.

But I know that things don't always go as smoothly in family businesses as they did in ours. And from what I have seen, there are a number of reasons for this. A friend of one of my brothers was in business with two of his brothers. One of the brothers didn't want to work as hard as the other two and would take a lot of time off to play golf. And when his kid came into the business, which was a relatively small business, he wanted his kid to get a big salary and other things he hadn't earned. There were constant arguments and after years of anguish, the business finally failed and each went their own way.

In another situation I am familiar with, two brothers, who were related to my late wife, took over the business when their father died. It was a great little business with a strong position in a small niche market. It was very profitable and both brothers were living very comfortably off it and were also doing well on the side with real estate investments. Then the wife of one of the brothers died and he remarried. His new wife began pushing him to get more from the business because he was the business getter while the other brother just ran the inside. This ended up in arguments and lawsuits, and the business was eventually sold and the families no longer talk to one another.

In yet another situation I know, the father controls everything. Two of his sons are in the business. One of the sons had no experience at all when he joined the company but was immediately made a vice president in charge of one area of the business. Unfortunately, he has an MBA from one of the prestigious universities and had the ego to go along with it, so he felt he knew everything he needed to know about the business. This really aggravated the older brother, who has worked in the business for some time. As a result, there were constant battles. To make matters worse, the father holds all the purse strings, paying each of his sons a basic salary and then giving bonuses based on need, not on individual or corporate performance. So if one son was getting married and wanted a new house, he got a bonus, and so on. I can't imagine a worse concept.

I could probably go on and on about horror stories involving family businesses. But there are many family businesses, like ours, that run very well. However, even many of those businesses eventually run into family troubles as future generations with varying skill levels and differing values come into the business, and as new family members and new spouses with streaks of jealousy and greed enter the picture.

But then that is the way of the world. Literature is filled with such stories. Kingdoms have fallen because of such family failings. The good news is that you now know that it absolutely can work extremely well. So if you are in or get into a situation where it isn't working well, my advice is to get a competent outside advisor, and there are plenty of good ones around, and try to set up the right situation. A good family business is too precious an asset to throw away without a hard fight to preserve it.

Did you know that family businesses employ more people than all the publicly held companies put together? They account for more of the economy of the United States. They also are the seedbed that nurtures and grows large companies. But more importantly, for the individuals running family owned businesses they can be great; you just have to make sure that the focus of the family owned business remains the business.

# Chapter 27

# The Glory of the Free Enterprise System

One of the greatest and most important proponents of the free enterprise system in the United States was born in Nevis, in the British West Indies, as an illegitimate child to a woman scorned by many. He was orphaned at fourteen, left with no money, and largely educated himself. He immigrated to the United States in 1772, rose to be a general and wartime adjutant to George Washington, and later became Secretary of the Treasury. To quote from the biography *Alexander Hamilton* by George Chernow, " . . . Hamilton, who was the prophet of the capitalist revolution in America . . . possessed the finer sense of economic opportunity."

In short, Alexander Hamilton set the machinery of capitalism in motion just as he set the mold for all the immigrants who followed him, who start with very little and build their fortunes, based on their initiative, their hard work, and their ability in this great land of ours where free enterprise and capitalism still are very much alive, in spite of the attempts by so many to hamper and destroy them. He set the stage for me, at twenty-six, to start an office supply business with $2,000 borrowed from my father-in-law and a phone in my dad's chicken store and, with the help of my two brothers, to build it into a more than $630-million-dollar company with more than 1,200 employees before we sold it 43 years later.

Based on historical record, the capitalistic, free enterprise system is the only one that works. In no other system do humans have the freedom to achieve to their fullest potential. And the entrepreneur is the essence of this system.

One day as I was looking out the window of my home at the gardens, lawn, and natural wooded area behind it, they made me ponder the landscape of our entrepreneurial system. With all the care they get, the lawns still get some weeds and brownouts. Bugs and deer get to some of the more formal gardens. Some of the expensive and carefully planted and maintained evergreens have branches that die or get too overgrown and begin to choke one another out. And some of the huge old trees, even in the open lawn area, have branches that die out and need to be cut off.

And once you get into the natural old wooded area, there is total disarray among the natural beauty. When we first bought the property, some of the big old trees, some as much as 75 feet high, had to be removed because they were dead. On others, dead limbs had to be removed. The forest floor was littered with old, rotting wood. And, in the shade of some of the big old trees, young trees that had taken root from seeds dropped by the old trees were growing—some of them, some day would grow to magnificent stature while others would not, some even dying early.

The capitalistic, entrepreneurial system is *not* a neat, tidy system. Indeed, communism was an attempt to create a neat tidy system—and we can see how that worked. In our system, there are those who succeed and those who fail. But in the end, everyone wins because it's a system that brings the most benefits to the most people. Just imagine, every entrepreneur out there is trying to figure out how he/she can provide people with what they want at a price they want to pay. They are competing with others to do it better and better in order to stay ahead of the fierce competition. No one has ever devised a better way of making life better for so many. And, indeed again, that's why communism was such a failure; there was no incentive for anybody to work any harder, or to do anything better than anybody else. Working hard for the good of the state just doesn't motivate anybody.

And yet, in our society, in our schools, there are so many who think the free enterprise system is wrongly conceptualized or implemented. In too many schools, school committees have tried to eliminate any trace of competition in the supposed protection of self-esteem. In that effort, they want to hold back or punish those who can achieve a great deal so those who can't, or don't want to try, don't have their self-esteem damaged. It's a strange concept and one that doesn't work in the hurly-burly of everyday life.

Our government itself throws up huge roadblocks in the form of a myriad of unfathomable laws and a crazy quilt of taxation. Every person in the United States is probably unknowingly breaking dozens of laws every day, laws they never knew existed.

But in spite of it all, the highly competitive free enterprise system thrives in the United States simply because human nature is what it is. There is, and always will be, people who want to be their own boss, people who are willing to bet on their own abilities and drive, people who are willing to take a chance on themselves. These are the people who are and who will be the entrepreneurs that make our economy (and our country) the best in the world.

To end this chapter, I would like to quote the ten "you cannots" by the Rev. William J.H. Boetcker, a Presbyterian clergyman and pamphlet writer written in 1916.

"You cannot bring prosperity by discouraging thrift.

You cannot strengthen the weak by weakening the strong.

You cannot help the wage earner by pulling down the wage payer.

You cannot further the brotherhood of man by encouraging class hatred.

You cannot help the poor by destroying the rich.

You cannot establish sound security on borrowed money.

You cannot keep out of trouble by spending more than you earn.

You cannot build character and courage by taking away man's initiative and independence.

You cannot help men permanently by doing for them what they could do and should do for themselves."

You may think it strange that I include this quote in a book on entrepreneurship because you may think that so much of it has little to do, directly, with being an entrepreneur. But I think it has everything to do with being an entrepreneur. I believe that every entrepreneur has an obligation, a sacred obligation, to defend and to perpetuate the system and the type of society that has given them the wonderful opportunity to be an entrepreneur—the opportunity to succeed and to go as far as their ambitions, their abilities, and their drive will take them. No man or woman can legitimately ask for more.

So I wish you good luck in your entrepreneurial efforts. Your success will not only help you and your family, but it will cascade out to help many others—and your country.

# Index

**A**

Accountability, as core value, 127

Accountants, value of, 203–205

Adams, Paul, 120–121

Advisors, 203–208
    accountants, 203–205
    bankers, 205
    board of, 207–208
    lawyers, 206–207
    weighing advice of, 201

*Alexander Hamilton* (Chernow), 215

*Alice in Wonderland* (Carroll), 58

Amazon.com, 66

AOL, 64

AON Corporation, 48

Arrogance of success, 64–66

Art of survival, 185–190
    "how to kill a business" examples, 186–189
    keys to survival, 189–190
    planning for hard times, 185–186

Attorneys, 206–207

Autism, 62

Automobile industry, 79, 112

Averages, in industry:
    financial statements and, 107–108
    forecasting and, 102–103

**B**

"Bag of Tools, A" (poem), 4

"Balanced life," entrepreneurs and, 30–31

Balance sheet, review of, 107

Banks/bankers, as allies in business, 11–12, 38, 205

Better ways, importance of finding, 79–83. *See also* Change

Blockers, getting rid of, 134, 141–142

Board of advisors, 207–208

Boetcker, Rev. William J.H., 217

Bonuses:
    forecasting and, 101, 103
    organization-building and, 140–141
    strategic goals and, 92

Buddha, 26

Budgeting and forecasting,
99–104
business survival and, 189
making adjustments in,
103–104, 105
at Quill, 101–103, 104
sharing of financial information and, 103
usefulness of, 101, 104
value of projections, 37,
99–100
"Burn out":
hard work and, 47–48
signs of, 165–168
"Burn rate," of capital, 40
Businesses, societal contribu-
tions of, 50. *See also* Free
enterprise system, value of

C
Canada, 192–193
Candy store syndrome, 86
Capitalism, value of, 71,
215–218
Carnegie, Andrew, 64
Cash flow, ways to improve,
42–45
Change:
consequences of failure to
respond to, 173–174
opportunities and, 174–178
Chenault, Ken, 68
Chernow, George, 215
Chrysler, 79
City of Hope, 187

Clausewitz, Carl von, 91
Collection time, improving of,
43–44
Compensation packages,
organization-building and,
137–138. *See also* Bonuses
Confidence, value of, 28–29, 57
Conner, Bart, 69
Control of business, financing
and, 37–38, 40
Core business, focusing on,
64–70
Core competencies, focusing on,
200
Core values, of Quill, 123–128
Corporate culture, 117–132
institutionalizing of, 128–129
intentional development of,
117–119
mission statements and,
119–120
rules to live by and, 122–124
Cost-cutting:
arguing with success and,
112–116
corporate culture and, 119
customer service and, 72,
76–77
at Quill, 23–24, 112–113,
115–116
at Successories, 113–116
Crate and Barrel, 68–69
Creative destruction, 112,
175–176, 178
Critical success factors, 129–131

Customer service:
aspects of, 74–75, 77–78
benefits of great, 71–78
as core value, 124
as critical success factor, 130
fanatical, at Quill, 13–14,
    24–25, 54–56, 72–73,
    76–77
in mission statement, 120
today's lack of good, 2–3, 33

**D**
Deadwood, getting rid of, 134,
    141–142, 201
Debt, staying free of, 40,
    185–187
Decision making, 29
Delegation, time management
    and, 149–151, 155
Dickens, Charles, 133
Direct mail, Quill and, 14,
    16–21, 80
Discounting, by Quill, 12,
    22–23, 175
Distractions, avoiding, *see*
    Focus
"Doing more by doing less,"
    159–164
"Don't want to/don't need to do"
    lists, 147–148

**E**
Ego, business survival and,
    190
Employee relations law, 206

Employees, *see also* Hiring;
    Organization, building of
    winning
enabling of people as core
    value, 125–126
importance of respect for,
    134, 140
involving in cost-cutting,
    112–115
involving in forecasting and
    budgeting, 101–102
providing support for, 3, 14
sharing financial information
    with, 106–107
Entrepreneurs:
characteristics of, 6, 27–32
free enterprise system and,
    218
risk and two types of, 10
Entrepreneurship:
easier today, 2–3
simple test for success at, 47
*Essay on the Principle of
    Population* (Malthus), 53
Estate planning, 206–207
Execution, *see* Implementation
Experience, learning from
    others', 1–2, 181–182, 191.
    *See also* Mistakes

**F**
Failure, *see also* Experience;
    Mistakes
avoiding fear of, 10–11
implementation and, 93–95

Family, making time for,
    49–50
Family business, 209–214
    business survival and,
        188–189
    reasons for tensions in,
        213–214
    values and, 210–213
"Fanatical," use of term, 3
FedEx, 79
Financial statements, 105–109
    forecasting and sharing of
        information, 103
    importance of regular review
        of, 106–109
Financing:
    methods of, 36–40
    strategic choices about,
        40–45
Firing, of deadwood, blockers,
    and malcontents, 134,
    141–142, 201
Fiscal responsibility, as core
    value, 126–127
Flat organization, 143
Fleet Boston Financial, 65–66
Focus, 3, 61–70. *See also*
    Strategic planning
    business survival and,
        187–188, 200
    core competencies and,
        64–70
    critical success factors and,
        129–130
    hard work and, 48

resources and, 63–64
talent and, 61–63
vision and, 59
Food service industry, 83
Ford Motor Co., 79
Forecasting, 99–104
    budgeting and, 100–101
    making adjustments in,
        103–104, 105
    at Quill, 101–103, 104
    sharing of financial
        information and, 103
    usefulness of, 101, 104
    value of projections, 37,
        99–100
Foreign competition, better ways
    and, 83
Free enterprise system, value of,
    71, 215–218
Future, *see* Vision

G
General Motors, 79
Getting started, 33–38
    acquiring knowledge, 35
    choosing business, 33–35
    financing and, 36–38
    talent and temperament and,
        35–36
Growth, of business, 190
    realism and, 200–201
Growth, of leader, 165–171
    warning signs of lack of,
        165–168
    ways to increase, 168–171

## H

Halas, George, 158
Hamilton, Alexander, 215
Hard work:
 as core value, 125
 necessity of, 30–31, 47–51
 time management and, 154
Heraclitus, 176
Hiring:
 fundamentals of, 134–138
 of good administrator, 149
 of talented employees, 31–32
 time management and, 163
Horders office supplies, 175
Hubbard, Elbert, 99

## I

Implementation, 91–97
 simplicity and, 95–97
 strategic goals and, 91–95
Industry averages:
 financial statements and,
  107–108
 forecasting and, 102–103
Information:
 flow of, 180
 gathering of, 80
Integrity, as core value, 127–128
Inventory turns:
 business survival and, 187
 improving of, 42
 review of, 107–108
Investments, business focus and,
  69–70. *See also* Retained
  earnings

## K

Knowledge, value of, 35

## L

Labor relations, 139
Lawyers, 206–207
Leader, growth and, 165–171
 warning signs of lack of,
  165–168
 ways to increase, 168–171
Learning:
 as core value, 124–125
 as critical success factor, 130
 importance of leaders',
  165–171
 value of, 27–28
 value of lifelong, 179–183
Life, control of, *see* Time
  management
Lifelong learning, value of,
  179–183
Lincoln, Abraham, 53–54
Lombardi, Vince, 124
Low-cost production, as critical
  success factor, 130–131

## M

Mail order business, Quill and,
  14, 16–21, 80
Malcontents, getting rid of, 134,
  141–142
Malthus, Thomas, 53
Management, corporate culture
  and, 118–119
Manual, for employees, 139

Marketing, as critical success factor, 130
Marshall Field, 81
MCI World Com Conferencing, 157
Medical supply business, 87–88
Meetings:
    increasing productivity of, 157
    time management and, 150, 155–157
Mergers and acquisitions, lack of focus and, 64–66
Micromanagement, avoiding, 159–164
Miller, Arnold:
    continual learning and, 181
    division of responsibilities and, 32, 210–212
    joins Quill, 10, 20, 39
Miller, Audrey, 13, 49
Miller, Goldie, 62
Miller, Harvey:
    continual learning and, 181
    division of responsibilities and, 32, 210–212
    hard work and, 49
    joins Quill, 10, 12, 14, 39, 179
Miller, Judy, 69
Mission statement:
    customer service and, 77
    importance of, 63
    of Providence St. Mel, 120–121

of Quill, 119–120
    strategic planning and, 89
Mistakes, 191–202. *See also* Experience; Failure
    at Quill, 191–193
    at Successories, 195–199
    tips for avoiding, 200–201
Monitoring of activities, 134, 142–143
Montgomery Ward, 79, 112, 173

N
Niche, *see also* Focus
    importance of finding, 26, 33–35
    strategic planning and, 86
"No," learning to say, 149–150

O
Office Depot, 21–22, 34, 64–65
Office Max, 21–22, 34
Office superstores, 5, 21–25
"Old truths," 3
Organizational structure:
    S corporation, 204
    success and, 142–145
Organization, building of winning, 113–145
    high standards and, 134, 140–141
    hiring and firing and, 134–138
    leaders' growth and, 169
    monitoring of activities and, 134, 142–143

removing deadwood,
blockers, and malcontents,
134, 141–142
respect for people and, 134,
140
structure choice and,
143–145
training and, 134, 138–140
Outsourcing, 177–178

**P**
Partners, value of good,
31–32
Payables, 44
Pension plans, avoiding,
137–138, 203
Perot, Ross, 29
Personal accountability, as core
value, 127
Peter, Lawrence J., 119
Planning, *see* Strategic planning
Plateau of business, as danger
sign, 166–167
Prioritization, time management
and, 150, 153–158
Private equity funding, 36–37,
39–40
Private label products, 175
Profit and loss statements,
review of, 107
Profits, putting back into
business, 40–42, 185–186,
189
Profit sharing plans, 137–138,
203–204

"Program of the month"
syndrome, 92–93
Projections, value of, 56, 196
Promotions, of employees,
136–137
Providence St. Mel, 120–121
Public companies, time required
to report on, 196

**Q**
Quill Office Products:
core values of, 123–128
corporate culture of, 117–132
cost control and, 23–24,
112–113, 115–116
critical success factors of,
130–131
customer service and, 13–14,
24–25, 72–73, 76–77
discounting and, 12, 22–23,
175
financial statements and,
106–107
forecasting at, 101–103, 104
history and growth of, 5–25
implementation of strategy
at, 93–95
mail ordering and, 14, 16–21,
80
mission statements and,
119–120
mistakes at, 191–193
organizational structure of,
144–145
private labels and, 175

Quill Office Products (*continued*)
  risk and, 10
  rules to live by of, 122–124
  sale of, 5, 10, 65
  strategic planning and,
    85–86, 88–89
  superstores and, 5, 21–25
  vision and, 54–58

**R**
Reagan, Ronald, 134, 142
Reavis, Isham, 53–54
Receivables:
  invoicing and, 13
  reducing of, 42–44
  review of, 108
References, checking of, 135
Reliable office supplies, 64–65
Reports, time management and,
    150, 155–157, 163
Resolve, future success and,
    53–54
Resources, focus and, 63–64, 189
Results-orientation, as critical
    success factor, 131
Resumes, interpreting of, 135
Retained earnings, 40–42,
    185–186, 189
Returns, processing of, 73
Risks:
  caution and, 200
  entrepreneurs and, 10,
    29–30
  vision and, 57
Rope theory, 68

Rules of business, changes in:
  consequences of failure to
    respond to, 173–174
  opportunities and, 174–178
Rules to Live By, of Quill,
    122–124
Ryan, Pat, 48

**S**
Santayana, George, 191
Sargent, Ron, 65
Schumpeter, Joseph, 175–176,
    178
S corporation, 204
Sears, 79, 112, 173
Segal, Gordon and Carol, 68–69
Self-service stores, 81
Self-starting, 31
Seneca the Younger, 158
Significant few, focusing on, 87
Simplicity:
  implementation of strategy
    and, 95–97
  strategic planning and, 86
  value of, 12–13
Smith, Fred, 79
Spouses, business survival and,
    188–189, 212
Standards, setting high, 134,
    140–141
Staples, 22, 34, 80
  business changes and,
    174–175, 177
  Quill and, 5, 10, 65
Steel industry, 83

Stemberg, Tom:
   mass merchandising and, 80
   origins of Staples and, 21,
      174–175, 177
   Quill and, 65
Strategic planning, 85–89
   cardinal rules of, 86–88
   implementation tactics and,
      91–95
Structure of organization:
   S corporation, 204
   success and, 142–145
Success:
   arrogance of, 64–66
   critical factors of, 129–131
   organizational structure and,
      142–145
   value of "arguing with,"
      111–116
Successories:
   core business and challenges,
      67–68
   cost control and, 113–116
   mistakes at, 195–199
Supervisors, training of, 139
Survival, art of, 185–190
   "how to kill a business"
      examples, 186–189
   keys to survival, 189–190
   planning for hard times,
      185–186

T
Talent:
   focus and, 61–63

getting started and,
   35–36
Target, 112
Teaching software, mistakes
   with, 194–195
Teamwork, as core value,
   126
Technology, better ways and,
   79–83
Temperament, getting started
   and, 35–36
Terms of payment:
   for payables, 44
   for receivables, 43–44
3M, 75–76
Time management:
   avoiding micromanaging,
      159–164
   delegation and, 149–151
   learning and, 182
   lists and, 147–148
   prioritizing and, 153–158
Time Warner, 64
Titles, avoiding too many,
   143–145
Training, organization-building
   and, 134, 138–140
Trust, verification and, 134,
   142–143

U
United Parcel Service, 79
Unwavering integrity, as core
   value, 127–128
Utility office supplies, 175

**V**

Values
  core values of Quill, 123–128
  family businesses and,
    210–213
Venture capital, 36–37, 39–40
Viking office supplies, 64–65
Vision, 53–59
  Quill Office Products and,
    54–58
  shaping of future with, 53–55
  sharpening of focus with, 59

**W**

Wal-Mart, 112, 173
"Want to/must do" lists,
    147–148

Ward, Aaron Montgomery,
    173
Waste, eliminating:
  business survival and, 188
  cash flow and, 44
  presence of waste and, 24
  time management and, 155
Work, *see* Hard work

**X**

Xerox, 79–80

**Y**

"You cannots," 217

**Z**

Zook, Chris, 66–68